MUSICAL NOTES
OF A
PHYSICIAN

F. William Sunderman, M.D., Ph.D., Sc.D.

1992

Library of Congress Cataloging–in–Publication Data.

Sunderman, F. William.
    Musical Notes of a Physician / F. William Sunderman.
    Revised edition.
    ISBN 0–9632927–0–6

Library of Congress card number: 92–81735

*To
Martha–Lee*

Preface

This collection of musical notes comprises radio addresses given in behalf of the Philadelphia Orchestra Retirees and Friends; adaptations from four lectures presented at the College of Physicians of Philadelphia, Section on Medical History; adaptations from illustrated lectures given at several Library Hours at The Union League of Philadelphia; and presentations at Gettysburg College. The musical program notes were originally prepared for the chamber music concerts of the Performing Arts Society of Philadelphia and the Sunderman Chamber Music Foundation series at Gettysburg College.

It is reasonable to believe that a musical composition, and especially a string quartet, reflects the inner spirit and character of the composer. "As one thinketh in his heart, so is he", – and the same concept applies to composing music. In these musical notes, I have endeavored to portray the spirit of the composer and his compositions from the viewpoints of both player and auditor. Since I have played and heard all of the works innumerable times (exceptions: Ginistera, Webern, and Kempff), a certain kinship gradually develops over the years which I have tried to depict in these brief essays.

My deepest gratitude is expressed to my dear Martha–Lee for her enthusiastic, eximious help. She undertook all of the typing and played a major role in the organization and editing.

F. W. S.

April 1992

Table of Contents

F. W. S. engaged in his daily practice in the wilderness of Yemen.

MUSINGS OF A PHYSICIAN
AND
AMATEUR CHAMBER MUSIC PLAYER[1]

Since concepts about chamber music among non–musicians are ofttimes vague, it has been suggested that for the furtherance of this form of music, an endeavor should be made to clarify some of the nebulous impressions about it. Accordingly, a brief résumé is presented concerning the historical development of modern chamber music, and an allusion is made regarding the enjoyment and benefits that might be derived from pursuing it as an avocation.

As a physician who has always been interested in the pursuit of classical music, I find myself in happy company with many other physicians having a similar interest. It perhaps should not be unexpected to find physicians absorbed in the dual fields of medicine and music. The noblest conception within the range of Greek mythology placed Phoebus Apollo as the god of both medicine and music. There is no doubt in my mind that the study of music aids in the study of medicine. The study of one appears to potentiate the other. Billroth, the distinguished Viennese surgeon, amateur musician, and intimate friend of Brahms, summed up his feeling in this matter with the statement:

It is one of the superficialities of our times to see in art and science two opposites. They are sisters, and imagination is the mother of both.

---

[1]Adapted from a radio address presented for the Philadelphia Orchestra Retirees and Friends.

Chamber music, as we are accustomed to think of it today, started in the Middle Ages when small groups of amateur musicians played for the court aristocracy. The term may include any combination of instruments (strings, keyboard, woodwind, or brass); however, in view of my interest in violin playing, emphasis will be pointed toward the area of chamber music for strings. By the seventeenth century, a number of composers (Buxtehude, Byrd, Corelli, Torelli, Vivaldi, Purcell, Eccles, and many others) were writing specifically for small string ensembles with separate parts for each instrument. Gradually, in the succeeding century, composers were encouraged to write music for four string instruments consisting of two violins, viola, and cello. This combination became known as the string quartet. Haydn was the most prolific composer for this medium with 83 quartets to his credit. Although other composers made notable contributions, it is generally acknowledged that to Haydn belongs the glory of being the "Father of the Modern String Quartet." Haydn's contribution rests mainly in the adoption of a polyphonic style in which the first violin ceased to be the dominant voice.

Chamber music for strings may include works from *duos* to *dezettes*; however, the string quartet continues to remain the most common and popular form. Beethoven, Schubert, Schumann, Mendelssohn, Brahms, and Dvořák wrote some of their best music in this medium. If asked to describe the salient characteristics of the string quartet as a form of artistic expression, one might summarize by classifying it as a form of group music that is graciously aristocratic and sophisticated with a reverence for beauty.

Such a characterization would seem to be a logical sequence, since many of the celebrated quartets by the great masters were composed for and first performed in the European courts and then later dedicated to the ruling princes of the land.

The evolution of the string quartet did not occur by sheer happenstance. It would not have evolved had not the means of expression been created through the genius of the Italian violin instrument makers. It is doubtful that chamber music could have ever reached its present stature if the instrument makers of Cremona, Brescia, Milan, Venice, Turin, and Naples had not worked so assiduously to produce the means for beautiful musical expression. The tone of the Italian string instruments in master hands has been difficult to equal or surpass. In the development of chamber music, these instruments became a necessity as an interpretative vehicle for the performance of the great musical works that were composed during the eighteenth century.

In addition, the new design of the bow contributed significantly to the enhancement of musical expression. In the judgment of the eminent conductor and musicologist, Theodore Thomas, the development of modern symphony orchestras and string chamber music ensembles would not have been possible were it not for the invention of the inverted arched bow through the genius of the French bowmaker, François Tourte (1747–1835).

Ever since college days, chamber music has been for me the most appealing form of music for listening and the most demanding for playing. In many ways, the demands for playing chamber music are greater than that of solo

3

performance. The chamber music player must acquire techniques for instantaneous adjustments and achieve high degrees of flexibility. I have on one occasion played with a renowned artist who had played the Sibelius violin concerto flawlessly the previous week with one of the major symphony orchestras and yet who had much difficulty reading and playing accurately the phrases of the Mozart *D Minor Quartet*. In a string quartet, the various musical items are distributed among performers so that at any given moment a player may be a soloist or an accompanist. Therefore, each part must be fitted together like a mosaic and must be subtly bound with each player contributing toward a musical balance. For satisfactory performance, string quartet players must weld themselves into a homogeneous unit. It is the mastery of such ensemble playing that offers an endless challenge and, if done well, generates the joy of accomplishment.

Many musical enthusiasts prefer the intimacy that chamber music provides to that of the larger musical forms in which the rapport between performers and audience is lost in the large concert hall. It is also noteworthy that most chamber music players would rather play themselves than listen to others.

In all of my adult life, I have found it to be relaxing beyond measure to set aside the perplexing problems of the day and to make music with congenial friends in the evening. Part of the exhilarations that come from ensemble playing is the sparkling conversations that usually develop during quartet sessions. These frequently pertain to the composers' lives; the circumstances under which the compositions were written; the differences of opinions about the technical skills and musical interpretations of outstanding performers on the different instruments; the merits of the instruments, bows, etc. All of such topics are remote from the labors of the day. However, when the evening's playing is over, the players are usually refreshed with beautiful melodies floating in relaxed minds and, as a consequence, they are better prepared to solve the problems of the morrow.

In a number of ways, group music, which is in reality chamber music, aided substantially in the development of our country. The hardy settlers pushing westward under the intrepid leadership of such valorous men as Daniel Boone, Lewis and Clark, usually took fiddles with them "to make light the heart and merry the soul." The early settlers were scattered and lived isolated lives, but after a while the fiddle brought them together for socializing with dance and song. Keen historians have observed that the early settlements became communities when people assembled in schools and churches to listen to music or just to fiddle together in groups.

Dr. F. William Sunderman Sr. and his son,
Dr. F. William Sunderman Jr.,
playing the Mozart unaccompanied *G Major Duo (K. 423)*
for violin and viola in Carnegie Hall, New York,
February 29, 1992.

MEDICINE, MUSIC, AND ACADEMIA[1]

Because of my personal associations in medicine, music, and universities, it seemed appropriate to focus this discussion upon three areas of interest. It is hoped that these areas might hold some appeal to you.

First, reference will be made to the contributions to music by three eminent physicians who lived during the past century, – namely Helmholz, Borodin, and Billroth. The second area will be directed to the furtherance of music through the friendship of Billroth and Brahms. Billroth was one of the world's greatest surgeons, and Brahms was one of the world's greatest composers of music. And, lastly, a resume of Brahms' *Academic Festival Overture* will be given in order to capture the spirit of the European universities about a hundred years ago.

CONTRIBUTIONS OF PHYSICIANS TO MUSIC

The art of music and the priesthood of medicine have been closely linked since ancient times. Greek mythology recognized the kinship of medicine and music. Although music and medicine have been closely related for thousands of years, nevertheless, at no time was the association more intimate than during the latter part of the past century in the European universities.

---

[1]Adapted from two published lectures given before the Section of Medical History, The College of Physicians of Philadelphia, *i.e.*, Medicine, Music and Academia, *Trans. Coll. Phys.* 27:140–147, 1969; Theodore Billroth as a Musician, *Bull. Med. Library Assoc.* 25:209–220, 1937.

In assessing the development of music during the past century, mention should be made of the outstanding contributions of three physicians, all of whom were contemporaries covering the period of 1821 to 1894, all of whom were professors in medical colleges of European universities, and all of whom were dedicated to the furtherance of music. These three physicians were Helmholtz, Borodin, and Billroth.

The first physician to whom tribute should be paid was Hermann von Helmholtz (1821–1894).

Hermann von Helmholtz.

Helmholtz possessed one of the greatest scientific minds of the nineteenth century and held professorships in the medical colleges of the Universities of Konigsburg, Bonn, Heidelberg, and Berlin. While at the University of Konigsburg, he published his monumental work entitled *The Sensations of Tone as the Physiological Basis of Music.* This book has been translated into many languages and is still fittingly referred to as the "Principia of Acoustics."

The second Aesculapian to whom honor should be given is Borodin,[1] the great Russian biochemist and professor in the Medical College at the University of Saint Petersburg during the past century. Alexander Porfirivich Borodin (1833–1887) was the illegitimate son of one of the Russian princes. The name, "Borodin", was the surname of one of his father's slaves. (One should, perhaps, realize that illegitimacy does not preclude one from attaining high honors in either music or medicine.)

Alexander Porfirivich Borodin.

---

[1]Refer to page 29 for a résumé of Borodin's life.

ON THE

SENSATIONS OF TONE

AS A PHYSIOLOGICAL BASIS FOR THE

THEORY OF MUSIC.

BY

HERMANN L. F. HELMHOLTZ, M.D.

FOREIGN MEMBER OF THE ROYAL SOCIETIES OF LONDON AND EDINBURGH,
FORMERLY PROFESSOR OF PHYSIOLOGY IN THE UNIVERSITY OF HEIDELBERG, AND NOW
PROFESSOR OF PHYSICS IN THE UNIVERSITY OF BERLIN.

TRANSLATED WITH THE AUTHOR'S SANCTION FROM THE THIRD GERMAN EDITION,
WITH ADDITIONAL NOTES AND AN ADDITIONAL APPENDIX,

BY

ALEXANDER J. ELLIS,

B.A. F.R.S. F.S.A. F.C.P.S. F.C.P.

PAST PRESIDENT OF THE PHILOLOGICAL SOCIETY, MEMBER OF THE MATHEMATICAL SOCIETY,
FORMERLY SCHOLAR OF TRINITY COLLEGE, CAMBRIDGE,
AUTHOR OF EARLY ENGLISH PRONUNCIATION, AND ALGEBRA IDENTIFIED WITH GEOMETRY.

LONDON:

LONGMANS, GREEN, AND CO.

1875.

"Principia of Acoustics".

10

Although Borodin was a distinguished scientist, his claim to immortality arises chiefly from his accomplishments as a musical composer which he himself regarded "as a recreation, a past–time, and an avocation that distracts me from my principal activity as a professor." Borodin founded the famous Russian Kouchka (Circle of Five)[1] whose members openly revolted against the rules and conventions of European music, feeling that the traditional classical music inhibited the free expression of Russian musical thought and feeling. Borodin did not leave a great number of compositions; what he did leave has weight and commands respect. Several years ago it was my miraculous good fortune to have rediscovered in Moscow, by sheer happenstance, Borodin's string sextet which had been lost since its initial performance in Heidelberg in 1863.

The third disciple of Hippocrates deserving of special tribute is Theodor Billroth (1829–1894), who was destined to become one of the outstanding leaders of his century in the development of both of the fields of medicine and music. Unlike Helmholtz, whose musical contributions were directed mainly to scientific considerations, or to Borodin, the talented composer of music, Billroth was both a physician and a musician whose musical contributions were mainly those of a philosopher, educator, mentor, and patron of the art.

Most physicians are well aware of Billroth's contributions to the medical science. His book on surgical pathology (*Allegemeine Chirurgische Pathologie und*

---

[1]The members of the Kouchka were Moussorgsky, Rimsky–Korsakoff, Cesar Cui, Balakireff, and Borodin.

Theodor Billroth.

Therapie) is still regarded as one of the finest treatises in medical literature, evidence by the fact that it has been translated into nine languages. Of Billroth's boundless energy, originality, and foresight in surgery, every surgical amphitheater in the world offers ample proof. However, the fact that he was a proved musician, that he wrote a book on the physiology of music (*Wer ist Musikalish?*), that he exerted a dominant influence on the music of his period – and especially the music of Brahms – is less well known, not only by physicians but also by musicians. But, this is a fact.[2]

---

[2]Brahms composed three string quartets, two of which he dedicated to Billroth. These quartets are frequently played in my home. Upon reading the dedication to Billroth on the title page of the *Opus 51* quartets, it is surprising how often accomplished musicians will ask, "Who was this fellow, Billroth, anyway?"

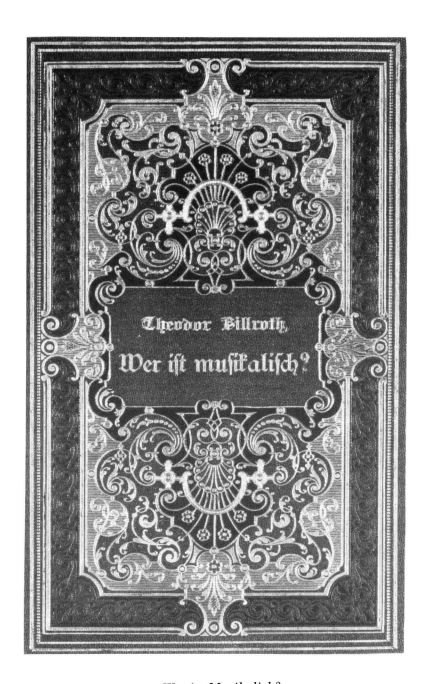

Wer ist Musikalish?

13

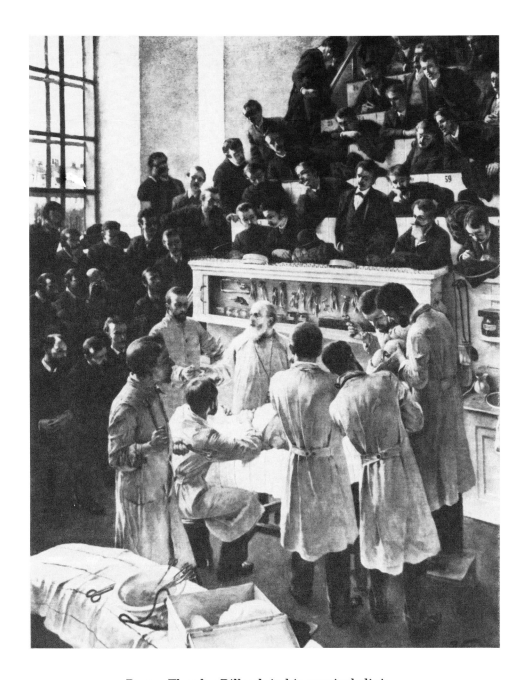

Doctor Theodor Billroth in his surgical clinic.

BILLROTH AND BRAHMS

This brings us to another area of interest, – the musical friendship of Billroth and Brahms.

During the early part of the last century, two boys were born in northern Germany about 125 miles apart. One boy was born in 1829 into a gracious, cultured home on the enchanting island of Rugen in the Baltic. He was the son of a Lutheran preacher and a descendant of four generations of distinguished scholars, artists, and musicians. The other boy was born four years later in 1833 into the uncultured environment of the slum district of Hamburg. He was the son of a poor, destitute musician, and his family filled a comparatively lowly position in life. The first boy became one of the world's greatest surgeons whose surgical operations with minor modifications are still used in almost every hospital in the world; the second boy became one of the world's greatest composers of music whose music is heard in practically every concert hall. The first boy was Theodor Billroth; the second boy was Johannes Brahms.

Theodor Billroth was gifted in music from his early youth. His maternal grandparents had been professional opera singers, and, through them, he became familiar with the compositions of the great masters. During his youth, he developed into an excellent pianist. At the age of nineteen, at the request of his family, Billroth gave up the pursuit of music as a career and began the study of medicine at the University of Göttingen. Although he was a student of medicine, nevertheless, at Göttingen he continued to keep up his musical interest and, on occasion, served as the accompanist for Jenny Lind and other artists.

Compared to the early career of Billroth, that of Brahms was quite dissimilar. In Brahms' early youth, two interested music teachers recognized the highly gifted talents of Brahms and furthered his musical education, in spite of his lack of facilities and financial support. He attended grade school and educated himself for the most part by voracious reading and diligent study. As a means of livelihood, he played dance music for the sailors and their girl friends in the brothels along the waterfronts of Hamburg. At the age of nineteen, he left Hamburg on a concert tour as the piano accompanist to the well–known Hungarian gypsy violinist, Remenyi. In the course of this tour, he had the good fortune to meet Robert Schumann, the composer, who proclaimed Brahms to be the coming musical genius of Germany. After concertizing extensively as a pianist, Brahms accepted the position as director of the School of Music in Detmold, Germany. Brahms composed some of his finest chamber music while holding this post.

Brahms in his study.

I am happy to have visited Detmold on a number of occasions, and while there I have always reserved Room 5 in the Hotel Stadt Frankfurt where Brahms lived from 1857–1859. Indeed, I feel a certain gratitude that some of my own ancestors emanated from this richly cultural area. When I visit Detmold, it also gives me pleasure to wander along the path through the Teutenberger Mountain to the Hermann monument at its summit. It was along this path that Brahms is said to have obtained the inspiration for a number of his most beautiful melodies. In spite of his prolific writings, at no time did Brahms ever gain a living from the sale of musical compositions. He sustained himself almost entirely by conducting orchestras and choirs and from appearances as a concert pianist.

After his Detmold days, Brahms returned to his home town of Hamburg and, deep in his heart, craved to be appointed the conductor of the Hamburg orchestra. When this position, however, fell to another, Brahms left Hamburg and settled in Vienna, a city comfortably administered by the Hapsburgs and glowing with the warmth of musical tradition.

Several years prior to the time that Brahms removed to Vienna, Billroth had accepted the professorship of surgery at the University of Zurich (1858). While at Zurich, Billroth developed an aversion for Wagner's music; however, the music of Brahms appealed to him. Thus it was with genuine delight that Billroth met Brahms, probably for the first time, in Zurich when the latter was on a concert tour. The account of Brahms' reception by Billroth is recorded in one of Brahms' letters to Clara Schumann:

> You may be able to gather how well I was received from the fact that after my first concert in Zurich. . . one or two musical friends. . . arranged a private concert on Sunday. . . . They hired the orchestra and telegraphed far and wide for the musical scores. . . . Anybody who had any interest in music was invited to listen without further ado.

In 1867, when Billroth was offered the Professorship of Surgery at the University of Vienna, he readily accepted. The acceptance was probably made more gladly since his friend, Brahms, had already moved to Vienna the previous year. He and Brahms had found much in common in Vienna. Both were North German Protestants transplanted to a foreign soil which was predominantly Catholic, and both maintained a strong patriotism which the war of 1866 helped to intensify. After the first three months in Vienna, Billroth wrote to one of this friends that within two months, he had attended nineteen concerts, had seldom gone to bed before two o'clock in the morning, and that he, Brahms, and Hanslick (the music critic who was also Professor of Music at the University) had met several times a week to attend a concert, go to the theatre, or simply to dine together. Billroth became enraptured with the musical nd artistic life of Vienna, but felt that in science he missed the strict German discipline to which he had been accustomed. In Billroth's words,

> Science requires a firm and hard ground rather than a rich, warm soil.

In Vienna, Billroth's home was simple in design, with the exception of the music room, which was ornate. At the innumerable concerts given at his home, Billroth was always the center of attraction. The audience seemed to be inspired by his striking image, his buoyant spirit, his glowing love of life, and his joy in making music.

Practically all of the chamber music composed by Brahms after 1867 was played for the first time before a selected audience in Billroth's home. Hanslick humorously remarked that Billroth had *"Jus primae noctis."* Throughout the ensuing years, the new compositions of Brahms were given to Billroth in manuscript form for his comments. This was a flattering acknowledgment of the confidence which Brahms place in Billroth's musical judgment.

The evening activities in Billroth's home were essentially of two types: those at which string quartets and the leading artists of Europe would perform informally before a small group and those before a larger group at which a formal concert would be given and Brahms would conduct. The guests for these occasions were proposed by Billroth, but no invitations were extended without Brahms' approval. After the performance, there was no difficulty in ascertaining Billroth's reaction. If the artists performed creditably, champagne was served with the refreshments; if the performance was mediocre, beer was provided. (I hope that this account will also merit a satisfactory libation.)

In the environment of Vienna and its great university, Billroth and Brahms remained loyal and devoted friends for more than a quarter of a century. Although Brahms held no academic appointment at the University, he became closely affiliated with it through his faculty associations and his posts as conductor of various musical organizations. The publication of 331 letters between Billroth and Brahms (many of which I have translated) affords an excellent portrayal of the cultured environment of Vienna and gives an insight into the dominant role that these men played in the furtherance of music during this past century.

With advancing years, Billroth became the idol of the University and the Viennese people. Although Billroth (in a letter to Brahms) expressed pleasure over his popularity, nevertheless, in a more critical letter to one of his former colleagues in Zurich, he wrote:

> What do the people really know as to my scientific accomplishments? Nothing. A myth develops: the myth starts from something not understood, partly from superstition, and develops into a miracle through the imagination of the people. I believe that the surgical removal of the larynx and replacing it with an artificial one was the beginning of the myth about me. The people have a morbid curiosity and the press knows well how to take advantage of it. Now, this would all be very entertaining, but I am overwhelmed by the profuse admiration.... What I know, my students know also, and perhaps even better.... At my years, I can be regarded only as a useful direction–pointer, – one who can point to the right way or at least in the direction to the right way.

It might be mentioned that almost all of the chairs of surgery in the leading medical colleges of Europe were occupied by Billroth's students.

The dominant passion throughout Billroth's life was his love of music. He believed that the study of music greatly aided his ability as a surgeon. Even in his medical writings, one senses the interest which Billroth had in music and musicians. Thus, in discussing methods for selecting men who are best fitted for university professorships, he quotes Schumann's maxim, "Perhaps only the genius quite understands the genius." One of the best illustrations of his tendency to write in musical terms is a letter written to his old Professor Baum at Göttingen:

The end of your letter in which you speak about your age in a sad tone does not agree with your otherwise youthful attitude.... The inspiration of living lies in the beautiful harmonic sequence of our major and minor thoughts. You have still plenty of time to think of the closing symphony of life as it is portrayed by Beethoven in the end of *Egmont* and in the *Ode to Joy* in Beethoven's *Ninth Symphony*. May God still keep you long as a conductor of the orchestra and have patience with one of the oldest members in your orchestra who is a violinist and is anxious to be advanced to the first stand.

At Billroth's death, the entire city of Vienna went into mourning. No ruling monarch was ever accorded more reverend respect. Brahms commented that, among the enormous crowd in attendance at the funeral, there was not one indifferent or inquisitive face but only expressions of deepest sympathy and affection. The stature of Billroth, the physician and musician, perhaps can best be appreciated by quoting a brief portion of the lengthy eulogy given by the rector of the University:

For Theodore Billroth, the black flag of mourning is flying from the roofs of official buildings. It signifies the death of a man who was the foremost ornament of our faculty. Science has lost one of its most genial representatives, an inspiring spirit at whom all of us younger men gazed in veneration.... The Vienna Medical School, all of Austria, and all of the world mourns this irreplaceable loss.... When he refused the call to the professorship of surgery in Berlin, he received from us an ovation which was a storm of enthusiasm and love. His words on that occasion still ring in our ears, when he said, "I cannot conceive that I would ever say farewell to Vienna." Now, we shall have to accustom ourselves to the thought that we have lost forever this scholar, this musician, this Samaritan, this thinker, this poet, and in one word, this genius — Theodor Billroth.

ACADEMIC FESTIVAL OVERTURE

In endeavoring to capture the unique spirit of commencement time at the European universities during the past century, attention has been directed to the University of Vienna in which Billroth, Brahms, and

Hanslick (the professor of music) dominated the medical and musical disciplines. It seems to me that this spirit is fittingly expressed in the music of Brahms' *Academic Festival Overture*. The *Academic Festival Overture* is mentioned in at least one of the letters of Brahms to Billroth, and it can be inferred that Brahms discussed the material and construction of this work with his devoted friend, Billroth.

The *Overture* was written in 1880 by Brahms as a gesture of thanks to the University of Breslau upon the conferment of an honorary degree. Thus, we see that this *quid pro quo* for honors was effectively applied in university dealings even a hundred years ago. In composing the *Overture*, Brahms did not make the customary formal approach, but based it upon the point of view of student tradition. The work involves the music of four time–honored student songs which, with the exception of one, were joyously sung at graduation and other festive occasions.

The first song in the *Overture*, which is brilliantly intoned by the trumpets, bears the title, *Wir hatten gebauet ein stattliches Haus* (*We Had Built a Stately House*). It is said that some of the student parodies were slightly ribald and would suggest that at least some of the houses build were not always in the character of stately mansions. The translation of the first verse is as follows:

> We had built a stately house,
> Inside of which we placed our trust in God,
> In spite of weather, storm, and fear.

The second student song is the *Landesvater* (the most solemn song to the Father of the Country).

Wir hatten gebauet ein stattliches Haus
(We had built a stately house)

Mäßig und innig.

Thüringische Volksweise. (1819)

1. Wir hat-ten ge-bau-et ein statt-li-ches Haus und drin auf Gott ver-trau-et trotz
2. Wir leb-ten so trau-lich, so ei-nig, so frei; den Schlech-ten ward es grau-lich, wir
3. Sie lug-ten, sie such-ten nach Trug und Ver-rat, ver-leum-de-ten, ver-fluch-ten die

1. Wet-ter, Sturm und Graus,— und drin auf Gott ver-trau-et trotz Wet-ter, Sturm und Graus.
2. hiel-ten gar zu treu!— den Schlech-ten ward es grau-lich, wir hiel-ten gar zu treu!
3. jun-ge grü-ne Saat,— ver-leum-de-ten, ver-fluch-ten die jun-ge grü-ne Saat.

Hochfeierliche Landesvater
(Most solemn song to the Father of the Country)

Feierlich.

Einer.   Vom Chor wiederholt.   Einer.

1. Al - les schweige! je-der nei-ge ernsten Tö-nen nur sein Ohr! Hört, ich sing' das
2. Deutschlands Söh-ne, laut er-tö-ne eu-er Va-ter-lands-ge-sang! Va-ter-land! du
3. Hab' und Le-ben dir zu ge-ben, sind wir al-le-samt be-reit, ster-ben gern zu

Vom Chor wiederholt.

1. Lied der Lie-der, hört es, mei-ne deutschen Brü-der, hall' es wie-der, fro-her Chor!
2. Land des Ruhmes, weih' zu dei-nes Hei-lig-tu-mes Hü-tern uns und un-ser Schwert!
3. je-der Stun-de, ach-ten nicht des To-des Wunden, wenn's das Va-ter-land ge-beut.

23

The *Landesvater*[5] song was written before 1770 and was used on rare occasions of patriotic consecration. A sword was passed around among the students in a fraternity, and each student pierced the sword through his colored fraternity cap, singing:

Ich durchbohr den Hut und schwore, halten will ich stets auf Ehre, stets ein braver Bursche sein. (I pierce the hat and swear I will always insist upon honor and always be a brave fellow.)

After the ceremony, the sweetheart was honored with the task of closing the hole in the hat by embroidering a silver oak leaf over it as a token of participation in a *Landesvater*.

The third song is the *Fuchslied* which literally translated is *Fox Song*. A "fox" in the German universities is an uninitiated freshman fraternity man. The song is a rollicking, jolly *roundelay* used in freshman initiation ceremonies. In the ceremony, the freshman entered the room riding on a heavy leather upholstered chair. The rumbling rhythm of this ride is well–marked in the instrumentation.

The melodies of these three songs are interwoven in the first part of the *Overture*. In using folk music, a composer cannot move abruptly from one song into the next but must employ bridgings.

---

[5]The full text of this song was obtained through the kindness of one of my friends who is a professor at the University of Heidelberg. I might say, parenthetically, that in preparing the material for this chapter, I am in the position of Charles Lamb who explained how he wrote one of his essays. Said he, "I milked twenty cows to get the milk, but the butter I churned is all on my own."

Fuchslied
(Fox Song)

Volksweise. (Bei Hall' ist eine Mühl'.)

Lebhaft.

1. Was kommt dort von der Höh', was kommt dort von der Höh'? was kommt dort von der
2. Es ist ein Po-stil - lon, es ist ein Po-stil - lon, es ist ein le-der-ner
3. Was bringt der Po-stil - lon, was bringt der Po-stil - lon, was bringt der le-der-ne

1. le-der-nen Höh', ça ça, le - der-nen Höh', was kommt dort von der Höh'?
2. Po-stil - lon, ça ça, Po-stil - lon, es ist ein Po-stil - lon.
3. Po-stil - lon, ça ça, Po-stil - lon, was bringt der Po-stil - lon?

Gaudeamus igitur
(Now, Let us be Joyful)

Alte Melodie. (1788)

Feierlich.

1. Gau-de-a-mus i - gi-tur, ju-ve-nes dum su-mus; post ju-cun-dam juven-tu-tem,
2. U - bisunt qui an-te nos in mundo fu - e - re? Va - di-te ad su-pe-ros,
3. Vi - ta no-stra bre-vis est, bre-vi fi - ni - e - tur; ve - nit mors ve - lo-ci-ter,

1. post mo-le-stam se-nectu-tem nos ha-be-bit hu - mus, nos ha-be-bit hu - mus.
2. tran-si-te ad in-feros, u-bi jam fu - e - re, u-bi jam fu-e - re.
3. ra-pit nos a - tro-ci-ter, ne-mi-ni par-ce - tur, ne-mi-ni par-ce - tur.

cresc.

25

The closing or fourth student song is the well–known *Gaudeamus Igitur (Now Let Us Be Joyful)*. This was and remains the official anthem of the German university student.

In composing the *Academic Festival Overture*, Brahms played the first three songs against each other in a most delightful way, and, after a recapitulation of all of the material, he had the orchestra burst into a highly–spirited jovial version of the celebrated *Gaudeamus Igitur* in which the students joined wholeheartedly in the singing. The translation of the fourth verse of *Gaudeamus Igitur* is as follows:

> Raise we, then, the joyous shout:
> Life to Alma Mater!
> Raise we, then the joyous shout:
> Life to Alma Mater!
> Life to each professor here,
> Life to all our comrades dear,
> May they leave us never,
> May they leave us never,

Brahms liked to refer to the *Academic Festival Overture* as his laughing or happy overture. He was criticized for pitching the *Gaudeamus Igitur* too high. This song is usually sung in either the keys of A Flat or B Flat. In order to achieve brilliance, Brahms raised the pitch to the key of C. So, excepting for the sopranos and tenors, one may find the orchestral version a little high for singing.

For the *Academic Festival Overture*, Brahms employed the largest orchestra he had ever used in any of his compositions. At the end of the *Overture*, he has every player scraping, blowing, and hitting as hard as he can.

The story of the *Academic Festival Overture* could be written entirely around Brahms. However, how much of the composition is really Brahms, and how much of it is Billroth? Certainly the happy festive character of the piece is more in keeping with the genial, extroverted personality of Billroth. Moreover, Brahms never attended a university as an undergraduate student and obviously had never taken part in a student fraternity initiation or in a *Landesvater* ceremony. Therefore, the student songs that were incorporated into the *Overture* would not have been as meaningful to Brahms as to Billroth, who had spent his entire life amid academic surroundings.

It is a matter of record that Brahms discussed the composition with Billroth, and, undoubtedly, there was an exchange of ideas concerning it. The exchange of ideas and the mingling of men's thoughts are ennobling forces that enrich the intellectual aura of every college or university environment. This exchange provides the inspiration for research and creative endeavor, and, as a consequence, it ofttimes becomes difficult (and really unnecessary) to give appropriate credit. However, the question might reasonably pose itself into an inquiring mind: Does the *Academic Festival Overture* emanate mostly from Brahms or mostly from Billroth? And then the second question should be asked: Does it really matter?

The names of Helmholtz, Borodin, Billroth, and Brahms and their monumental works will doubtless live through the ages. The last movement of Brahms' *German Requiem* was based upon a verse from *Revelations* which the pastor also used as the text at Brahms' funeral:

Blessed are the dead which die in the Lord for henceforth they may rest from their labors and their works will follow them. (*Revelations* 14:13.)

27

Alexander Porfirivich Borodin.

ALEXANDER PORFIRIVICH BORODIN

PHYSICIAN, CHEMIST, AND COMPOSER

In the *Lancet* of 1887, there appeared an obituary of the physician and chemist, Alexander Porfirivich Borodin, which, after outlining briefly his eminent scientific career, closed with this casual statement:

> He is, indeed, said to have rendered valuable service to the cause of music in Russia.

Now, after the passing of a century, the fact that Borodin had been a distinguished laboratory physician who had received recognition throughout the world is almost forgotten; his claim to immortality arises chiefly from his accomplishments as a musical composer which he, himself, regarded as

> . . . a recreation, a pastime, and an avocation that distracts me from my principal activity as a professor.

To Borodin, art and science were inseparable throughout his entire life, yet he found only an hour or so a day to devote to music and preferred to be known merely as a "Sunday" musician.

The birth year of Borodin is questionable. Though he may have been born in the year 1833, on his tombstone the year of his birth is recorded as 1834, On October 31, 1873, Eastern Calendar (November 12, Western Calendar), Borodin wrote, "Today is my fortieth birthday." On that same day, however, an old servant in his family told him he was only thirty–nine years of age. Borodin gladly accepted this assertion and never bothered to verify its correctness.

Alexander Porfirivich Borodin was the illegitimate son of Prince Luke Ghedeanof, a descendant of the last rulers of Emeretia, which was an ancient kingdom in the Caucasus. His paternal ancestors claimed to be descended from David and adopted the harp and sling for their coat–of–arms. His mother, Eudoxia Kleineke, was twenty–five years of age and his father sixty–two at the time of his birth. The child was given the name "Borodin", the surname of one of his father's slaves.

Borodin was reared in a pleasant maternal environment. His mother was cultured, beautiful, and financially independent. In youth, he was of such delicate physique that some of his relatives believed him to be tuberculous and advised his mother not to spend too much time and money on his education since, in their opinion, the expenditure would probably be fruitless. His mother, however, took exceptionally good care of him physically and, despite the advice of her relatives. she had him tutored in French, German, and music and gave him every educational advantage. Early in childhood, Borodin displayed a remarkable talent for music and, at the age of nine, composed a polka entitled *Helene* in honor of a woman living in his home. At the age of twelve, he received lessons on the flute and 'cello and began to express enthusiasm for the playing of chamber music. At this early period, he wrote a concerto for flute with piano accompaniment and also a string trio for two violins and 'cello.

During his adolescent years, Borodin became fascinated with the study of chemistry. The rooms in his apartment were filled with jars and beakers from which he prepared his own fireworks and water–colors. These boyhood leanings toward music and science later developed into the absorbing interests of his life.

At the beginning of the 1850s when Borodin was sixteen or seventeen years of age, a new era in higher education was evolving in which the study of science was beginning to be emphasized in the university curricula. Courses in chemistry and physics became popular with students and superseded to some extend those in philosophy and history. Encouraged by his mother, Borodin entered the St. Petersburg Academy of Medicine in 1850 and was soon attracted to the Academy's chemistry department, then under the direction of Professor Zinin. Although Borodin was naturally very shy, it did not require long for Zinin to appreciate his real enthusiasm for chemistry and to recognize in this youngster his own possible successor, whom later he accepted as an adopted son. As a student, Borodin was brilliant; the only criticism offered of his examinations pertained to his habit of quoting the Scriptures too freely.

Writing in the *Russian Journal of Physical Chemistry* in 1880, Borodin described the chemistry laboratory and Zinin, the professor who had such a profound influence upon his later life:

His [Zinin's] laboratory was the meeting place of young scientists who regularly came to visit with him. These young fellows were eager to share with Zinin the results of their experiments and to receive his advice, to discuss their ideas and plans, etc. His laboratory was transformed into a miniature chemistry club and meeting place where the ideas of the young Russian chemists were exchanged. Here Zinin in his high–pitched voice would explain enthusiastically the newer ideas and, for lack of chalk and blackboard, would write on the dusty table with his finger the equations of those reactions which have such an important place in the chemical literature.... I remember especially the

Monday evenings when there would be gathered a small but interesting group of scholars and scientists. In his small study there would be heated debates and discussions. At these gatherings, Zinin would display his intellectual power, vast knowledge, outstanding memory, keen and original humor.

It may be interesting to note that Zinin's outstanding achievement in science was his work that led to the preparation of aniline derivatives from aromatic nitro compounds and, thus, initiated the study of the chemistry of dyes.

Borodin's friends at the Academy were, in the main, not Russian students but Germans, whom, as a group, he considered more cultured and more interested in music. So many of their evenings were devoted to the playing of chamber music that Zinin, on one occasion, reproached Borodin, saying,

You would do better to become less occupied with your music. You know I am depending upon you to succeed me, but you are thinking only of music. You are making a mistake by chasing two rabbits at the same time.

After completing his studies at the medical school, Borodin obtained an internship at the Military Hospital in St. Petersburg where, for the first time, he met Moussorgsky, a young subaltern in one of the fashionable regiments of Russian guards. Moussorgsky, like Borodin, was also interested in composing music. By virtue of this mutual hobby, they became intimate friends.

The year following his internship, Borodin prepared a thesis on the analogy between arsenious and phosphoric acid and received a medical degree on May 3, 1858. He practiced medicine for only a short time after internship, since his interests lay in the academic aspects of medicine and especially in the fields of physiological and organic chemistry.

The year after graduation from medical school, Borodin went to Heidelberg to work in Erlenmeyer's laboratory with his Russian friend, Mendelieff. During the three happy years he spent in Heidelberg, Borodin began research work in organic chemistry and published several articles in English, French, and German chemical journals.

Borodin and Mendelieff spent their summer vacations largely in travel. Mendelieff describes their trips in a very vivid manner:

We would travel with light baggage – just a bag for the two of us. We wore blouses and tried to pass for artists, since in Italy this has financial advantages. We bought underwear on the way which later we would give to the waiters as tips. In this way we visited Venice, Verona, and Milan in the spring of 1860. In the fall of the same year, we visited Genoa and Rome. Near Verona our railway coach was searched by the Austrian police for an Italian who had been held as a political prisoner and who had escaped. The southern features of Borodin attracted the attention of the police who believed that Borodin was the fugitive whom they sought. They inspected our baggage and questioned us but found out that we were just poor Russian students and so left us alone.

We had scarcely crossed the Austrian border when one of our fellow passengers in the coach started to hug and kiss us and to shout "Evviva." The fugitive had really been in our group and had crossed the border without being recognized. Thus, thanks to the suspected features of Borodin, the fugitive had escaped the clutches of the Austrian government.

While a student at Heidelberg, Borodin met Catharine Protopopoff, who later became his wife. This girl, an accomplished pianist, had come to Heidelberg for a rest following a concert engagement in Moscow. Their mutual love of music and the fact that they were Russians living in a foreign country played a large part in bringing about their affection for each other. In her memoirs, Catharine wrote concerning their friendship in Heidelberg:

> He [Borodin] became like a brother to me, taking care of my health, my treatments, and even my financial affairs. Accompanied by a friend, R, I often went to Baden Baden to play roulette and would lose considerable money. . . . Borodin played quite a trick on me by pretending that he needed money and asking me to lend him almost all that I had. Since I could not easily refuse to lend him the money, I had to forego playing roulette. It was only much later that I learned that he had borrowed my money only to prevent me from losing it.

Borodin returned to the St. Petersburg Academy of Medicine in the fall of 1862 as an associate professor in organic (including physiological) chemistry, under Zinin, and as a professor of chemistry in the school of forestry. At this time, he began a series of researches on condensation reactions of aldehydes, which led to the discovery, later in life, of aldol (β–hydroxybutyric aldehyde), simultaneously with Wurtz in 1873.

Borodin's interest in music was more than a superficial drawing–room attraction, so that after returning to Russia he lost little time before resuming his studies in musical composition. Through his friendship with Moussorgsky, Borodin became associated with a small group of musicians who studied the technique of orchestration and the esthetics of music under Balakirev. Balakirev and Cesar Cui had been advocating for some time the introduction of nationalism in Russian music. Joined with them in their nationalistic aims were Rimsky–Korsakoff, a former naval cadet; Moussorgsky, the military officer; and Borodin. This small group which played such an important role in the advancement of musical composition during the past few decades became known as the "Kouchka" or the "Russian Circle of Five." It would seem significant that the "Kouchka" was composed essentially of men of science, Balakirev having been a mathematician, and Cui a professor of fortifications in the Engineer's Academy.

The "Kouchka" openly revolted against the rules and conventions of European music, feeling that traditional classical music inhibited the free expression of Russian musical thought. Their idea of nationalism in music was to treat folk songs with gay and brilliant flourishes, adorning them with the very artificialities which are the direct antithesis of folk music. This "Free School of Music", headed by Balakirev, searched for, and used mainly, liturgical chants and folk songs as their musical idiom.

Being a young professor, who was by nature reticent and self–conscious, Borodin was hesitant to confess his activities as a composer of music. He derived, however, much encouragement to continue in this work from the "Kouchka" and from the pianist, Liszt. Balakirev, in a letter to Stasoff (who later became Borodin's biographer) wrote:

Our union was exceedingly stimulating for Borodin. Up to that time he considered himself an amateur and did not regard his compositions as important. I was the first one to reproach him and he immediately began to compose his symphony in E Flat Major.

Just as Liszt had been one of the first Europeans to laud Wagner's contributions to music, so also he encouraged Borodin, advising:

Do not listen to those who wish to deter you. Believe me, you are on the right track. Your artistic instinct is such that you should not be afraid to be original. Remember that the same sort of criticism was given to Mozart and Beethoven in their time. If they had followed the advice of their critics, they would not have become great masters.

Cesar Antonovich Cui.

Nikolai Andreevich
Rimsky–Korsakoff

Modest Petrovich
Mussorgsky

Milii Alekseevich
Balakirev

After Borodin's marriage to Catharine Protopopoff in April, 1863, he moved his living quarters to the new chemistry laboratory where he remained as the director until his death. Here Borodin worked tirelessly throughout his life and was available at all hours to any student or associate who requested his help or advice. Those who worked in the laboratory were made to feel as though they were members of Borodin's family and never hesitated to approach him with questions and new ideas.

One of the most descriptive accounts of Borodin's home life may be found in Rimsky–Korsakoff's autobiography, from which the following excerpts are taken:

Of all my intimate musical friends, I visited Borodin the oftenest. . . . His inconvenient apartment, so like a corridor, never allowed him to lock himself in or pretend he was not at home to anybody. Anybody entered his [apartment] at any time whatsoever and took him away from his dinner or his tea. Dear old Borodin would get up with his meal or his drink half–tasted, would listen to all kinds of requests and complaints and would promise "to look into it.". . .

[His wife] continually suffered from asthma, passed sleepless nights, and [did not get up until] 11 or 12 o'clock. . . . [Alexander] had a difficult time with her at night, rose early, and got along with insufficient sleep. Their whole home life was one unending disorder. . . . Their apartment was often used as a shelter or a night's lodging by various poor [or "visiting"] relations, who picked that place to fall ill or even lose their minds. Borodin had his hands full of them, doctored them, took them to hospitals, and then visited them there. In the four rooms of his apartment there often slept several strange persons of this sort; sofas and floors were turned into beds. Frequently it proved impossible to play the piano because someone lay asleep in the adjoining room. . . .

Borodin was a man of very strong physique and health; a man of no whims and easy to get along with. He slept little, but could sleep on anything and anywhere. He could dine twice a day, or go dinnerless altogether, both of which happened frequently. Borodin would drop in on a friend during dinner; he would be invited to join the meal, – "As I have already dined today and, consequently, have formed the habit of

dining, I might as well dine once more." – Borodin would say and seat himself at the table. They would offer him wine, – "As I don't drink wine, as a rule, I might treat myself to it today." – he would reply. Next time it might be just the contrary.

Throughout his life, Borodin had an affection for cats and always kept several in his home. His mother would pay as much as 100 rubles for one that took her fancy. Rimsky–Korsakoff relates that if a guest were to brush away one of the cats that made for the guest's plate at the dinner table, Borodin's wife would invariably take the cat's part and tell some incident pertaining to the animal's biography.

Although Borodin and his wife had no children of their own, they took care of several. On one occasion, it is recorded an adopted daughter asked Borodin to play a piano duet with her. When Borodin asked of the child what she could play, she replied that she knew how to play Chop–sticks. Borodin then proceeded to write a polka to harmonize with the playing of Chop–sticks. This gave Rimsky–Korsakoff the idea of composing a set of variations on the Chop–stick theme. Cui and Liadof were also invited to contribute to the amusement. After the paraphrases were published, Liszt, in a letter written to a friend, praised them highly. The musical critics of St. Petersburg, however, were indignant over the publication of such a conglomerate musical composition and, when confronted with Liszt's favorable comments, they even doubted the authenticity of Liszt's letter. Later, Liszt, in order to emphasize the esteem with which he regarded these paraphrases, retaliated by composing a prelude which was published in the second edition of this entertaining work.

Typical of the easy manner with which Borodin handled delicate situations is the letter that he wrote to Rimsky–Korsakoff's son, aged two months!

Dear Sir: – Your Father lent me a horn to play. Now I am in a very difficult position. Your Father asked me to send it back as soon as possible, but your Mother, who dislikes all noisy toys, asked me to keep it as long as I could. Since I cannot please them both I am sending the horn to you. However, I find it necessary to tell you not to put the instrument to your mouth. It is made of brass. Excuse me for giving you such advice, but you are so young. I am older than you and therefore more experienced (and besides, I studied medicine). I know very well that young men of your age put everything that they find into their mouths. I had the same habit myself, but it really was a long time ago. Believe me that if I permit myself to give you such advice, it is due to my interest in you. My best regards to your Mother and Father. Sincerely yours,
Borodin.

Borodin published approximately twenty major articles on chemical subjects. In addition to his studies on the aldehydes, he prepared and studied the reactions of several organic fluorides and wrote a few papers dealing with some of the higher fatty acids. In his later years, he was occupied with physiological studies pertaining to nitrogen metabolism. He invented a nitrometer for the estimation of nitrogen in organic compounds which was widely used and described in most of the then current chemistry manuals.

In the 1870s, Borodin established himself as a pioneer in the cause of medical coeducation in Russia. He, together with Professor Roudneff and Mrs. Tarnovsky, founded the Women's Medical College of St. Petersburg in 1872. At this institution, Borodin served in the capacities of professor of chemistry and treasurer until his death.

Of Borodin's major musical compositions, twelve were published during his lifetime and nine were published posthumously. In 1875 he wrote to a friend:

> When I am so ill that I must stay at home and can do nothing important, my head splitting, my eyes filled with tears, so that every moment I must take out my handkerchief, then I compose music.

In another letter, he wrote:

> I must point out that I am a composer looking for something unknown. I am almost ashamed to confess to my composing activities. For others the composition of music is the goal of their lives. For me, it is only recreation, fun, which takes time from my serious business as a professor. I am absorbed in my work, my science, my academy and my students. Men and women students are dear to me.

It was the opinion of some of Borodin's colleagues, however, that his best musical compositions were written at periods when he appeared to be most active in the laboratory.

An intense national character predominates in Borodin's music. While manifest even in his first *Symphone in E Flat Major*, it does not reach heroic proportions until the second *Symphone in B Minor*, and the great epic opera, *Prince Igor*. The opera was begun in 1869 at the suggestion of his friend, Vladimir Stasoff, who believed that the story of the army of Igor would afford Borodin an inspiring patriotic medium for his talent. Borodin procrastinated dreadfully in writing the opera, and it is regrettable that he left it unfinished at the time of his death. His friends, Rimsky–Korsakoff and Glazunov, finally completed it in 1889. Concerning this procrastination, Kurbanoff wrote:

No persuasion of Borodin's close friends was of any avail. Everything seemed to stand in his way, and one restless, unsystematic day passed after another, giving him no time whatsoever for composing. Once I went over in the evening and Borodin was out. I was met by Dianin who told me how Rimsky–Korsakoff had just called and had wept and prayed before the ikons and sworn that the cause of Russian music was lost as long as *Igor* remained unfinished and as long as Borodin was entangled in trifling matters with charity organizations which could be done by anybody, while *Igor* could be completed only by him. Dianin added that Rimsky–Korsakoff's lamentations seem to have some effect on Borodin who had promised to attend to *Igor* – next summer!

That Borodin was not always in happy spirits and had many cares and worries is revealed in a letter written to his friend, Mrs. Karmolin:

Our Academy is awaiting its verdict. . . . There is much anxiety, unnecessary red tape and bad financial arrangements. This leaves me little time for my beloved work. At home things are not going smoothly. My poor wife is always sick and this year worse than last. The only thing that cheers me up is the Women's College. It takes lots of time, but gives me a moral satisfaction. On account of my work on all kinds of committees, etc., I have no time for my music. When I have time for physical relaxation, I lack the peace of mind which is so indispensable for composing music.

On February 15, 1887, Borodin wrote a letter to his wife, who was then living in the drier climate of Moscow on account of her health:

Tomorrow we shall have a dance. It is going to be a grand affair – a costume–ball in the auditorium. I do not care to write to you about it since others will tell you about it later.

This dance had been arranged by the professors of the Academy for their families and friends. Borodin attended, dressed in the costume of a Russian peasant. It is said that he was in an especially gay and lively mood that evening, – dancing, telling jokes, etc, when suddenly he leaned forward and dropped dead from a heart attack.

Borodin was buried in the Alexander Nevsky cemetery, next to Moussorgsky. His students carried the coffin on their shoulders from his home in the laboratory to the burial ground. Many obituaries were written after his death. A part of one published in the *Journal of the Russian Chemical Society* by his colleague, Dianin, is as follows:

Borodin was very human. He was always looking for an opportunity to help someone. He gave money, advice and assistance to any friend who asked him. In his later years when his memory was not so keen, he made notations on scrips of paper of the things he wanted to do. On one of these papers he wrote, "Go to B and ask him to admit A into a hospital. Write a prescription for K. Talk to B concerning D. Could not something be done for V." If he succeeded in helping someone, he was very happy.

In 1889, Borodin's friends erected an elaborate tombstone in honor of his memory. The design consisted of a bust of Borodin, embellished with inscriptions of the organic compounds which he had studied and of the main themes of some of his musical compositions.

Some years ago there appeared in French literature a psychoanalytical study of Borodin by LaCombe. This author endeavors to provide reasons for the fact that Borodin preferred to remain a "Sunday" musician and to follow a scientific rather than a musical career. LaCombe's analysis may be summarized somewhat as follows:

For Borodin science expressed no sentiments or emotions, whereas music was the embodiment of both. His teacher and foster father, Zinin, had encouraged Borodin to become a scientist and not a musician. Borodin could never forget that he had been an illegitimate child and, hence, his true father, whom he had never known, had in the deepest sense discouraged him from expressing his emotions. Being particularly gifted in music, Borodin was thus faced with a most difficult psychological situation.

Now, these many years after his death in 1887, those scientific activities which were Borodin's primary interests in life are, to a large extent, forgotten, while his music is becoming more widely known. In the words of Sir Henry Hadow:

No musician has ever claimed immortality with so slender an offering. Yet, if there be, indeed, immortalities in music, his claim is incontestable.

Tombstone of Alexander Porfirivich Borodin in the Alexander Nevsky Cemetery, Saint Petersburg, Russia.

44

Domes of Saint Nicholas Cathedral, Saint Petersburg, Russia.

Cathedral Tower
Cremona, Italy

STRADIVARI

250th Anniversary

 ntonio Stradivari da Cremona,
Sovereign genius through centuried time;
Whose viols enrich the Songs of Angels
To the most glorious sublime.

William Anderman,

46

ANTONIO STRADIVARI OF CREMONA

Many volumes have been written about Antonio Stradivari, who is overwhelmingly acknowledged by connoisseurs of string instruments to be the greatest violin–maker of all times. The fame of Stradivari is so great that his name has become legendary in the field of violin–making. As a master of his art, he stands on a level with Rembrandt and Michelangelo in painting and sculpture; with Beethoven and Bach in music; and with Shakespeare and Goethe in literature.

Antonio Stradivari was born in 1644 in Cremona, Italy, and spent his entire life in that town. His family was relatively wealthy. The name, "Stradivari", as translated from the Latin, means a "straddler of the road." This name was given to the family because for generations the family had been the toll–keepers in Northern Italy, a section then called Lombardy. The coat of arms of the Stradivari family tells of their work. The emblem depicts two sea horses going up a road and a bar across the road to simulate a toll gate.

The town of Cremona rests on the banks of the River Po, about fifty miles southeast of Milan. It was famous for making fine violins for over 350 years, from about 1550 to 1900. At present, the chief industry in this quiet, peaceful community is cheese manufacturing. During my travels, I have visited the town on a number of occasions in order to try to ascertain the type of environment that led to the development and work of the great Italian violin makers.

During recent years, the city of Cremona is renewing its interests in violin–making by maintaining a school for that purpose. Alfred Primavera, the son of Adolph Primavera of the House of Primavera here in Philadelphia, is a graduate of the Cremona School, following in the footsteps of his father. The Primaveras maintain a shop in Cremona where Alfred is presently making exceedingly fine instruments. Thus, through the Primaveras, Philadelphia has established a direct link with Cremona. It might be noted that during the golden period of violin–making in Cremona (*i.e.*, 1665 to 1765), it is estimated that more than 20,000 master violins were distributed throughout the world.

The outstanding violin–making school in Cremona in 1644, when Stradivari was born, was that of Nicolas Amati. The Amati shop undertook the training of apprentices. One can surmise from the records that the competition for admission to the Amati school must have been exceedingly keen. It is obvious that Nicolas Amati taught Stradivari the secrets of his school and furnished him with the patterns that he used for his early violins. However, it is only fair to state that there are no written records that Stradivari was an apprentice to Amati.

It was the custom of the time in the 1600s for the census takers to walk through the streets of Cremona and call in the front door of each house, "Who sleeps here?" A search of the records has indicated that the census takers never listed Stradivari as an apprentice in the house of Amati.

In the 1600s, boys between the ages of twelve and fourteen years became apprenticed to a master. It was the custom for apprentices to sleep in the house of their master. It is now generally agreed that Stradivari, coming from a wealthy family and living in the same diocese as Amati, would probably go to his home every evening to sleep in his father's house. However, there is no record of this either. Nevertheless, from the evidence of the early instruments of Stradivari, there can be no doubt that Amati was the teacher of Stradivari.

House of Stradivari in Cremona.

At about the age of twenty, Stradivari opened his own violin shop. At first he continued to make violins of the Amati pattern but soon became ambitious to develop his own patterns through a series of trial and error experiments. The contributions of Stradivari to the development of the violin were many. These include the lowering of the arches of both the top and the back to obtain flatter instruments than those of the earlier makers; a more careful shaping and design of the inner bouts; the standardization of the volume of the air in the violin chamber; and the artistic design of the F holes and scroll. The beautiful lustre of the varnish which Stradivari obtained has never been completely duplicated.

There is no record of the number of instruments that Stradivari made during his lifetime. The best estimates place the number at approximately 1,100. About 500 of these instruments have been authenticated and are listed in authoritative treatises on the subject. The *Iconography of Goodkind*, published in 1972, contains photographs of all the authenticated Stradivari violins up to that time. Stradivari worked actively making violins until his death in 1737 in his ninety–fourth year. In his later years, he annotated the year as well as his age on the label. Several years ago I had the opportunity of playing on the Strad in the possession of Sydney Harth, the concert violinist. On the label of this instrument, it was stated that the violin was made in his ninety–third year. When one recalls that Michelangelo produced some of his finest sculptures in his eighties and Stradivari, in his nineties, made some of his finest instruments, this may give comfort for achievement by senior citizens.

There were apparently no major paintings of Stradivari made during his lifetime. The only likeness of the master that has been preserved is a miniature medallion painted by Gialidini in 1691.

Medallion painted by Gialidini.

A verbal description of Stradivari's appearance was given by the violin virtuoso, Polledro (Turin, 1781–1853) who alleged that his teacher had known Stradivari personally and had described him as "a tall, lean man who wore a white woolen cap and, when working, a white leather apron." An artist's conception of Stradivari in his workshop is shown in the print.

Antonio Stradivari.

Stradivari was buried in the family vault in the Rosary Chapel of Saint Domenico's Church. The church became decayed and was torn down for the construction of another church. At that time, Stradivari's remains were committed to a common grave. The tombstone marker, however was preserved and placed in Cremona's town square.

To me, the real secret of Stradivari's success may be attributed to the fact that he was raised in a town at a time when it was deeply involved in violin–making and, therefore, he was in a competitive environment. Furthermore, he was undoubtedly taught by one of the greatest teachers in the craft. Early in life, Stradivari had apparently heeded the advice of Marcus Aurelius:

Love the little trade that thou has learned and be content therewith.

Moreover, Stradivari possessed the intelligence, the skill, the scientific reasoning, and the intuition to produce his masterful works of art.

It is really not very difficult to detect the instruments made by Stradivari. In the first place, throughout his life he used relatively few trees from which he made his instruments. As a consequence, the pattern of the grain can be scientifically detected. Stradivari learned early in life how to test wood for tonal qualities. When he found a good tree, he worked it to the end. At the centers of the top and bottom of all Strad instruments is a small wooden peg about one–eighth inch in diameter. These pegs are also found in the works of later masters. Also, Strad instruments have the so–called "bumble–bee stingerette." These stingerettes are present on each bout of the violin as a small hairline insert made of peachwood, which is placed from the end of the purfling to the edge. It is interesting to observe that Stradivari almost always placed his stingerettes off center. His artistic eye apparently could not tolerate the suggestion of mechanical uniformity.

A number of years ago, I was in Milan on a consulting trip for the chemical subsidiary of the Rohm and Haas Company. Our meeting concluded one morning at 11 o'clock, and the manager of the company noted that I was not scheduled to leave Milan until the following morning. He asked what would be the most hospitable thing that he could do for me. I responded by saying if he was in earnest, I would appreciate borrowing his secretary (who spoke

F. W. S. at site of Stradivari marker in Cremona, Italy.

English) and his chauffeur and automobile for an afternoon visit to Cremona. I had heard that a violin–making school had been started in Cremona and that it was proving to be an excellent technical training institute. The manager was most agreeable and stated that I should be ready to leave within twenty minutes. Fortunately, I had my Stradivari violin with me. When travelling abroad, I habitually keep my violin by my side.

Our trip from Milan to Cremona was uneventful. We had lunch and arrived at the school around 2 o'clock. I met the director, Mr. Sartini, who graciously suggested that we tour the institute. During our tour, I mentioned on two or three occasions that I had a Stradivari violin in the case which I was carrying with me. He seemed unimpressed. Finally, as we were ending our tour, I asked him if he would like to see the instrument. He replied, "Well, if you would like to show it to me." I opened the case, and he took one look and shouted in Italian to the apprentices, "Giovanni, Paulo, . . . Come quick. It is genuine!" Then he explained that there was seldom a month that someone had not visited the institute claiming that the violin case contained a Stradivari violin. The violins invariably proved to be spurious. However, the violin in my possession was the only one in which the instrument was genuine.

Mr. Sartini then explained that there had been no Stradivari violins in Italy for more than fifty years and, as a consequence, the city of Cremona purchased one from the famous violin dealer, – Hill of London. This violin was kept in the vaults of the Cremona Town Hall. Mr. Sartini then telephoned the Mayor and suggested that a celebration might be appropriate by bringing the two violins together. The Mayor was most agreeable.

Mr. Sartini, Director of the violin–making school in Cremona (left) is holding the Irish Strad (owned by F.W.S.) and comparing it with the Joachim Strad (owned by the Italian government) held by the Mayor of Cremona (right).

As we were leaving Cremona to return to Milan, Mr. Sartini told me that he was amazed that I was travelling about Italy unprotected. He stated that when Desmond Hill brought the Stradivari violin to Cremona, the city assigned day and night custodians to guard the instrument.

Several months ago in the course of casual conversation, a friend of mine made a statement that there was practically nothing in this world that had not undergone some type of revolutionary change in this century. I replied that I knew of at least one item that had not been fundamentally changed for over 400 years. That item was the violin as developed by Caspar DiSalo, the Amatis, Stradivari, and the early Italian masters.

You may wonder why I collect violins rather than other works of art, such as paintings. Unlike paintings, violins give double pleasure. One cannot only appreciate the beautiful craftsmanship of the instruments but enjoy playing them. They appeal both to the eye and ear. The early Italian instruments have a beautiful grace and elegance comparable to a Phidias carving.

A few words might be said about the construction of the violin. Basically, the violin has both the elements of art and the characteristics of science. In construction, it is essentially a hollow box about 14 inches long, 2 inches deep, and from 6–1/2 to 8 inches wide. It is composed of about 80 parts, each of which contributes to its beauty, strength, resonance, and tonal qualities. The instrument itself weighs only a little more than a pound, although it supports a string tension of 68 pounds and a pressure on the bridge of 28 to 30 pounds. The thinness of the shell is sometimes not realized. The range of graduation from the top to the back is 3/32 inch to 1/32 inch, – about the thickness of a half dollar. The thickest portion is in the center of the back, which is about 1/8 inch or about the thickness of two pennies. The strength of this thin, wooden shell lies in the shape of the arch, which is hand–carved (not bent) from the edges to the centers of the top and back.

In spite of the thin, wooden construction, the physical stamina of some of the old instruments is almost unbelievable. Even after 300 years of constant usage, the condition of many of them is excellent.

The question is often asked, "Just what do connoisseurs of string instruments see in an instrument to justify the soaring prices?" Many persons look for a logical background for high prices. To those persons, theoretically, a $100,000 violin should be demonstrably 100 times as good as one costing $1,000. However, that type of reasoning has no place in the minds of art dealers who have a way of bypassing rationalizations. It is that tiny edge of artistic superiority of old Italian instruments that inflates the prices. This is aided by the increasing rarity of the older instruments plus a fleeting, effervescent commodity known as "glamour."

May I close with this thought. Those of us who have treasured instruments should take care of them reverently and lovingly, – ever mindful of the fact that we are custodians with the responsibility for their care and maintenance and are entrusted to pass these treasures on to future generations.

The Reverend H. R. Haweis, in a lecture to the Royal institute in London in 1872, expressed this pertinent sentiment:

The violin is perennial. It grows old with its perpetual youth. There is no reason why it should ever wear out. It sings over the graves of many generations. Time, that sometimes robs it of a little varnish, has no power over its anointed fabric.

The hard, durable substance steeped in silicate–like varnish has well–nigh turned to stone, but without sacrificing a single quality of sweetness or resonance.

The violin is the only fossil which still lives, and lives with a fullness of life and a freshness that contrasts quaintly enough with the fleeting, sickly, and withering generations of man. Even should mishap bruise or break its beauty it can be endlessly restored. It is never fit for death; it survives a thousand calamities. . . .

Thus human in its power and pathos, superhuman in its immortal fabric, the violin reigns supreme, the king and queen of all instruments – and, in the hands of a Paganini, a Joachim, an Ernst, or a Sarasate, the joy and wonder of the civilized world.[1]

Coat of arms of the Stradivari family.

---

[1]Preface from the publication, *Old Violins* by H. R. Haweis.

Antonín Dvořák and his wife, Anna.

DVOŘÁK'S SOJOURN IN AMERICA

Some twenty years ago, I attended a one–week summer chamber music conference at the University of Hartford in which the members of the Stradivari String Quartet served as the course instructors. The members of the Quartet held faculty positions at the University of Iowa. At one of the conference recitals, the Stradivari Quartet included Dvořák's *American Quartet, Opus 96*, as one of its selections. William Preucil, the violist in the Stradivari Quartet, presented a brief review of the *American Quartet* and mentioned that Dvořák had composed it in Spillville, Iowa, in the summer of 1895. I became curious to know the background by which Dvořák composed this great work in chamber music in the remote midwestern town of Spillville. The following is a brief account.

Iowa was organized as a territory and opened for settlement in 1838 and was admitted to the Union as the 29th state in 1846. When Sylvester Mason, a prominent politician addressed the State's constitutional convention in 1846, he urged that the electoral franchise of the new state be extended to foreigners, stating:

They know better how to appreciate the inestimable blessing of liberty than we do.

The availability of abundant fertile farm land and immediate rights of citizenship made Iowa an attractive spot for settlement by Joseph Spielman, a Czechoslovakian revolutionary who was forced to flee from Bohemia after the unsuccessful revolution of 1848. Spielman arrived in Iowa in 1851 and was the first settler of "Spielville", Iowa, which soon became Americanized to Spillville.

61

Spielman built a saw mill on the banks of the Turkey River. He also attracted several families of Czechoslovakian refugees and emigrants to settle in Spillville, where they could converse in their native language and enjoy Bohemian culture in an atmosphere of freedom and serenity.

In 1860, nine years after the first settlement, the Bohemian Catholic Church of Saint Wenceslaus was erected in Spillville, – a truly magnificent structure for midwestern America of the time. Shortly thereafter, a

Saint Wenceslaus Bohemian Catholic Church, Spillville, Iowa.

Czechoslovakian organ was installed in Saint Wenceslaus Church, – the organ on which Dvořák was destined to compose the *American String Quartet* and four other compositions.

By 1869, the settlement had grown to 340 inhabitants, and the town fathers invited a young Czeck scholar and musician named Jan Kovarik to emigrate to Spillville to serve as organist and choirmaster of Saint Wenceslaus Church and to serve as schoolmaster of the village school.

Jan Kovarik singlehandedly transformed the frontier settlement of Spillville into one of the cultural centers of Iowa. He was the founder of the Spillville orchestra and band. His prize students of the violin included his nephew, John Bily, who became a prominent violinist in St. Paul, Minnesota, and his son, Joseph Kovarik, who served for many years, until his death in 1951, as principal violinist of the New York Philharmonic Orchestra. Joseph Kovarik had studied violin and viola at the Prague Conservatory of Music, and it was he who induced Dvořák to visit Spillville.

During the 1890s, Spillville became a center for many facets of Bohemian culture in addition to music. Wood carving and the construction of elaborate cuckoo clocks in the Bohemian tradition were carried on by the Bily brothers. A brewery was errected and the Nockles Brewery produced excellent Pilsner Bohemian beer throughout that decade.

At this juncture, mention should be directed to Antonín Dvořák's background. He was born of peasant stock in Nelabozeves, near Prague, in 1841. Dvořák's father was a butcher and an innkeeper. His mother had been a servant in the cultivated musical household of Prince

Bily Clocks, Spillville, Iowa

Lobkowitz (to whom Beethoven dedicated six string quartets). Dvořák demonstrated an interest in music in early childhood, and, despite poverty and privation and against the strong opposition of his father, Dvořák managed to acquire proficiency as an organist, violinist, violist, and, finally, as a composer.

At the age of 32, Dvořák married Anna Čermáková, a former pupil who was the daughter of a well–to–do goldsmith in Prague. Anna's steady encouragement, excellent musical judgment, and sound business accumen were invaluable for Dvorak's professional development. Dvořák's first success as a composer came at the age of 34 when he submitted a symphony to the Austrian Commission for State Music and was awarded a prize of 400 gold florins. Even more important, his genius was recognized by Johannes Brahms, who was one of the three judges. Brahms arranged for Dvořák's compositions to be performed throughout Europe and to be published by Simrock, the German music publisher.

Largely as a result of the friendship and encouragement of Brahms, Dvořák's career as a composer flourished. His compositions captured the nationalistic spirit of the Slavonic peoples and achieved wide recognition. During the 1880s, Dvořák's musical reputation grew steadily, owing to the enthusiastic critical acclaim of his *D Major Symphony* (1880); the publication of his *Slavonic Dances* and *Slavonic Rhapsodies* for piano (1878); the performance of his great oratorio, *Stabat Mater* (1877); and the performance of his superb violin concerto (1880).

Despite his increasing fame, Dvořák remained a simple, methodical peasant who conscientiously composed forty bars of music every day, or, as he stated, "about three hundred bars weekly." He was a devout Catholic, and a man of compulsively regular habits who went to bed every night by 9:00 P.M. His only hobby was a passionate interest in railroad locomotives which he was permitted to operate on occasion in Czechoslovakia.

Some measures of his recognition as a composer can be assessed by the fact that in 1890 and 1891, he was awarded an honorary doctorate of philosophy from Charles University in Prague, an honorary doctorate of music from Cambridge University in England, and he was elevated to membership in the Czechoslovakian Academy of Arts and Sciences. Moreover, in 1891 he was appointed Professor of Composition at the Prague Conservatory of Music.

At this time, an influential American woman, Mrs. Jeannette Thurber, was seeking a musician to serve as

Director of the National Conservatory of Music that she had established in New York City in 1855. Mrs. Thurber was the wife of a wealthy business man in New York and, through her philanthropies, sponsored many musical undertakings, among them the National Conservatory of Music. The Conservatory was a non–profit corporation, modeled somewhat after the Paris Conservatory. Mrs. Thurber envisioned in her new project the emergence of an American school of music composition. Accordingly, she sought as the director someone who had gained world–wide recognition as a composer, and her attention was directed to Dvořák in Czechoslovakia and Sibelius in Finland. After wide consultation, Mrs. Thurber decided that Dvořák was her first choice, and she sent an emissary to Prague to negotiate with Dvořák.

Dvořák was astounded by the offer of an annual salary of $15,000 and a two year contract to serve as the Director of the National Conservatory, with the stipulation that he would have official duties for only eight months during the year and four months of vacation! Despite distaste for the long sea voyage and for the protracted absence from his country, Dvořák and his wife decided that the offer was simply too attractive to be declined. Dvořák accepted Mrs. Thurber's offer and arrived in New York City in September 1892. He was accompanied by his wife, two of their six children, and by Joseph Kovařík, the Prague student from Spillville, Iowa, whom Dvořák had recruited to serve as his translator and secretary. Upon arrival, he immediately set to work to conduct a special concert on October 12, 1892, which Mrs. Thurber had organized in recognition of the 400th anniversary of Columbus' discovery of America.

The winter of 1892–1893 in New York City was extraordinarily difficult for Dvořák. His plain life–style was completely out of keeping with the sophisticated life of New York, and, furthermore, he annoyed Mrs. Thurber by his stubborn insistence of going to bed by 9:00 P.M. Dvořák found the National Conservatory to be haphazardly organized and entirely different from what he had envisioned. The music students were poorly disciplined, and the musical standards were inferior to those in Prague. Moreover, the locomotive engineers in America were not as friendly as they were in Czechoslovakia, and he was not permitted to tinker about locomotives. His only pleasures were daily walks in Central Park and the close friendships which he developed with some of his students, – particularly a talented negro named Harry T. Burleigh, who frequently sang negro spirituals for Dvořák's enjoyment.

When spring came, Dvořák longed for the companionship of Bohemian country folk and for the opportunity to converse in his native language. Therefore, it was only natural that he and his family would accept the invitation of Joseph Kovařík's father to spend the summer in the Bohemian colony in Spillville, Iowa. Needless to write that Dvořák was also pleased by the prospect of the long railroad trip to Chicago and thence to the tiny depot at Calmar, Iowa, seven miles from Spillville.

Antonín and Anna Dvořák summoned their remaining four children from Prague to join them for their summer vacation. On June 5, 1893, a party of eleven people – Dvořák and his wife, six children (Otilie, Aloisie, Magda, Anna, Antonín, and Otakar), his sister–in–law, a maid, and Joseph Kovařík arrived in Spillville where they enjoyed sumptuous accommodations on the second floor of a building which accommodated a bakery and a tinsmith on the first floor. In recent years, the building has served as a museum for hand–carved clocks made by the Bily brothers.

Dvořák and his family were immediately delighted with everything in Spillville. On the day after he arrived, Dvořák arose at 5:00 A.M. for a stroll along the Turkey River. He then attended 7:00 A.M. Mass at Saint Wenceslaus Church, where he surprised everyone by going directly to the organ and playing the Czech hymn, *O Lord Before Thy Majesty*. This delighted the entire congregation, which immediately joined in singing. He continued this routine throughout the summer. Dvořák spent almost every morning during his summer vacation improvising and composing on the organ. At other times, he strolled through the countryside, pausing to scribble a few bars of music on his cuffs, and stopping at one of the beer parlors to enjoy a liter of the splendid Bohemian beer and to converse with his friendly compatriots.

On the third day after he arrived in Spillville, Dvořák began to compose the *American Quartet*. He completed sketches of the entire work in the incredibly short time of three days. Harmonization of the score was completed on June 23, and Dvořák wrote on the last line of the last movement:

Thank God. I am satisfied. It went quickly.

The quartet was first played on June 23 by Dvořák as first violin; Jan Kovařík, the schoolteacher, as second violin; Kovařík's daughter, Cecilia, as viola; and Joseph Kovařík, who played cello on this occasion. Dvořák stated that the theme of the third movement was a transcription of

Organ in Saint Wenceslaus Catholic Church, Spillville, Iowa.

the call of the scarlet tanager, the bright red bird with black wings that delighted him during his morning walks along the Turkey River. Dvořák also included in the last movement of the quartet an imitative organ passage reminiscent of the hymn, *O Lord Before Thy Majesty*, as it sounded on the tiny organ in Saint Wenceslaus Church.

The summer that Dvořák spent in Spillville was the most productive period in his musical life. In addition to the masterful *American Quartet*, he finished a string quintet, *Opus 97*, and sketched most of the *New World Symphony*. On September 8, 1893, the townfolk surprised Dvořák by a festive birthday party at which they presented him with a magnificent hand–carved mantle clock that still ticks in his studio (now a museum) in Prague. In the middle of September, Dvořák discovered that his 15–year–old daughter, Otilie, was had fallen in love with a local farm boy. Enraged, he immediately packed up the entire family, and they all returned without delay to New York City.

The first public performance of the *American Quartet* was given on January 12, 1894, at Carnegie Hall in New York by the Kneisel Quartet and proved to be an immediate success. In contrast to the previous winter, Dvořák's second winter in New York was much more agreeable and musically profitable because of the great popularity of his *American Quartet*, the *New World Symphony*, and the *Humoresque* for violin and piano, – compositions on which he put the finishing touches soon after returning to New York City. Dvořák left New York on May 19, 1894, and returned to Vysoka, near Prague, on May 30, where the townfolk greeted him with a band and a lantern–lit parade which terminated with a great beer party at the local inn.

Home of Dvorak at 327 East 17th Street, New York City, New York.

Franz Peter Schubert.

SCHUBERT'S SERAPHIC SPIRIT[1]

This year marks the 150th anniversary year of Schubert's death on November 19, 1828. In musical circles, 1978–1979 is known as Schubert's year, and Schubert's music has been prominently programmed by major symphony orchestras, chamber music and choral groups throughout the world.

Franz Peter Schubert was born on January 31, 1797 in Vienna, the son of Franz Theodor Schubert, a parish schoolmaster, and Elizabeth Vietz. He was baptized on the day following his birth, and at the baptismal font was given the name of "Seraph."

Every work of Schubert might be classified as an early work, for Schubert lived only 31 years. Yet in the span of less than 15 years of writing, he composed melodies which, after 150 years, have continued to maintain world–wide popularity. It is probably safe to assert that no music is universally as much loved as is Schubert's.

Schubert portrayed more than music itself; he portrayed a romantic lyricism which poured forth so easily, clearly, freely, and unobtrusively from his creative mind. In 1818, he wrote from Hungary:

All is well with me. I live and compose like a god, as if it had to be so.

The furtherance of Schubert's genius was aided by the regal elegance, splendor, warmth, and beauty of Vienna in Schubert's time. In Schubert's era, Vienna indulged heavily in *Gemütlichkeit*, with dancing, drinking, love–making,

---

[1]Remarks by F. W. S. at the 150th Anniversary Memorial Concert for Schubert, Washington, DC, November 7, 1978.

chatting in coffee houses, and the giving of parties devoted to music making and the reading of romantic verses. Life in Vienna in the early 19th century represented a flood–tide of inhabitants in love with love.

At that time, Vienna was also the most beautiful of European capitals. Within its confines was the magnificent Ringstrasse with its double rows of trees, and within its gates, and a stone's throw of St. Stephen's cathedral, were the bohemian lodgings where Schubert lived. The Lobkowitz and Rasoumovsky palaces were also in the center of the city, and all were within walking distance to Belvedere and the Schönbrunn. The city was referred to as Biedermeier's Vienna.

Biedermeier was a cartoon character in a humorous journal called the *Fliegende Blätter*. This character composed verses called *Biedermeierlieder*. The name "Biedermeier" is applied to the Viennese period between 1800 and 1850 and connotes joviality, good fellowship, conviviality and *savoir–vivre*. Schubert was a classical representative of Biedermeier ease and comfort as well as that of a humble schoolmaster and fiddler. Portraits of Schubert show him always attired in the Biedermeier style of dress.

Schubert's nickname among his friends was *Schwammerl* (little mushroom) because of his small, plump appearance and good–natured smile. During his lifetime, Schubert was never a public figure. He was unknown as a performer and, excepting for his small group of bohemian comrades, he was relatively unknown as a composer. According to Hutchings:

He was the most modest of men to whom it can never have occurred that his was the next name in the apostolic succession of musical pontiffs to follow that of Beethoven.

During Schubert's lifetime, only a handful of his compositions were published or performed publicly, and Schubert's talents were not generally recognized. It may be noted, however, that Beethoven was aware of Schubert's great musical gifts. When Beethoven read the manuscripts of some of Schubert's songs, he said:

Surely, there is a divine spark of genius in this Schubert.

A decade passed after Schubert's death before his musical legacy began to be discovered.

Carole Geisler–Schubert, the composer's grandniece, writing upon Schubert's genius for happiness, stated that

Franz Schubert was one of the happiest morals that ever lived.

She expressed the wish that:

People should be encouraged to picture his dear, good merry face, instead of the gloomy pining features depicted by plaintiff historians. This sentimental, unmanly whining tone, so foreign to Schubert's brave, cheerful spirit, must be emphatically contradicted.

I can do no better in emphasizing Schubert's seraphic spirit than to quote the phrase attributed to the poet, Bauernfeld, that Schubert manifested a

. . . joyousness of heart with which God endowed him at his birth.

We shall all have an opportunity to witness this seraphic joyousness by listening to the Schubert music that is to be performed this evening.

Sir Thomas Beecham.

SIR THOMAS BEECHAM

Born in Saint Helens, Lancashire, on April 29, 1879, Sir Thomas Beecham was the son of Sir Joseph and grandson of Thomas Beecham, founder of the pill–making firm which bears their name. Displaying an early aptitude for and enjoyment of music, Sir Thomas was educated at Rossall School, Wadham College at Oxford, and in German universities.

His first public professional concert took place in the Town Hall, Saint Helens, in December 1899, when he conducted the Halle Orchestra at short notice at a concert given to mark his father's inauguration as mayor.

In a professional career spanning more than sixty years, Beecham formed four major orchestras. In 1911, he was responsible, jointly with his father, for bringing to England, for the first time, the Russian Opera and Ballet. He also introduced to England the operas of Richard Strauss. In the period between the wars, he produced and directed over 80 operas at the Royal Opera House. His championship of the music of Frederick Delius, whom he first met in 1907, was notable. He was an outstanding interpreter of the music of Berlioz, Brahms, Handel, Haydn, Mozart, Schubert, Richard Strauss, and Wagner, among others.

Beethoven's music did not appeal to Beecham. When I asked him on one occasion regarding his impression of Beethoven's last string quartets, he merely shrugged his shoulders and replied:

Well, Beethoven never heard them.

Beecham was made a Companion of the Legion d'Honneur for his services to French music. Knighted in 1916, he succeeded to the Baronetcy in the same year on the death of his father. Sir Thomas was also made a Companion of Honour. He appeared with most of the world's major orchestras, making his American debut with the New York Philharmonic Orchestra in 1928 and returned to conduct the Orchestra almost yearly. At the age of 70, Beecham took the Royal Philharmonic Orchestra on an extended tour of the United States. This was the first British orchestra to visit our country since 1912. The Orchestra gave 52 concerts in 64 days, – a remarkable feat.

After World War II, a number of German scientists were brought into our country to work on the moon rocket projects in Huntsville, Alabama. Several of them were excellent chamber music players, and, on my consulting visits to Huntsville, I usually arranged to play string quartets with them on at least one of the evenings of my sojourn. During these pleasant times, a couple of the Germans were fond of relating Beecham stories. One of them comes to mind.

The German scientists were first taken to San Antonio, Texas, for their initial research studies. During that time, San Antonio decided to put on a gala performance of *Aida*. Contracts were made for Beecham to conduct the opera, Metropolitan Opera singers were selected, and all of the ancillary requirements were obtained, including scenery and a live elephant. However, the acquisition of orchestra members to play the opera was overlooked. As a consequence, frantic efforts were made only a relatively few days before the opening to recruit musicians in and about the San Antonio area. Two of the German scientist–musicians were included in the final selections. Sir Thomas experienced great difficulty in molding a pick–up group composed mostly of amateur musicians into a presentable orchestra for the operatic production. Several rehearsals were scheduled. During the dress rehearsal, the elephant defecated on the stage. Sir Thomas stopped the orchestra and said:

Ladies and gentlemen. You will notice that the elephant disgraced himself, but do you not believe that we deserved it?

СЕКСТЕТ   SEXTET

А. БОРОДИН
A. BORODIN

I

М. 18267 Г.   3

First page of the score of the Borodin sextet.

80

IN QUEST OF CHAMBER MUSIC COMPOSITIONS

Today's social structures and artistic contributions have evolved, to a large extent, from the vestigial remains of the eighteenth and nineteenth centuries. This is particularly true of chamber music contributions. In my home where chamber music has been played one or two evenings each week for many years, it has been found to be instructive and entertaining to sight–read quartets from less well–known composers of past decades, – Donizetti, Miakovsky, Hummel, Glinka, Shebalin, etc. As a consequence, when visiting foreign countries I am fond of perusing music shops in search of unusual chamber music compositions. Occasionally, discoveries are made and worthwhile acquisitions are forthcoming. I was particularly fortunate on a visit to Moscow during the 1960s when I discovered the lost Borodin *Sextet*.

REDISCOVERY OF BORODIN'S SEXTET

Owing to my special interest in Borodin's life as a physician, chemist, musician, and composer, I sought to acquire, for my library, all of his chamber music works. From references in his published letters, I found that Borodin had written a string sextet during his days at the University of Heidelberg. However, the only comments that I could locate about the *Sextet* was in Cobbett's *Cyclopedic Survey of Chamber Music* (vol. 1, page 148):

In 1860, during a stay at Heidelberg, Borodin wrote a string sextet which was publicly performed there. The MS., which he presented to one of the Heidelberg musicians, is lost. Later, he described the work as "very Mendelssohnian in character, and written to please the Germans."

Catalogues of chamber music, such as that by Wilhelm Altman, fail to mention the composition.

During a visit to Moscow in 1962 to attend the International Biomedical Congress, I spent some of my free time visiting music stores. In one small store, when I asked to see the offerings in secondhand chamber music, I was directed to a musty basement and shown a stack of music published before World War I. I sat on an old box and sorted through the compositions for a couple of hours.

Near the bottom of the stack, I chanced upon the long–lost *Allegro in D Sextet* by Borodin. The paper of this work was somewhat deteriorated and appeared to have been printed on stone plates. It is doubtful that the music had ever been used. I presume that other copies were made, but in my research I have been unable to find evidence of their existence.

If I had not been familiar with Borodin's letters describing the *Sextet* and had not known that this composition was lost, my attention would not have been attracted to the manuscript. It was an inexpensively priced work. I purchased the battered manuscript at a cost equivalent to 35 cents.

Owing to stringent customs inspections, I requested the music store to mail my purchases to my address in Philadelphia. Evidently the Russian customs officials raised no objection to sending me the dog–eared score of a century–old composition, for the Borodin *Sextet* arrived in good condition a few weeks later. Needless to mention that copies were made of the *Sextet* and sent to the library of the

Moscow Conservatory as well as to music conservatories and important music libraries in our country.

The New York Sextet frequently included the Borodin *Sextet* in their nationwide performances and graciously gave recognition to my discovery.

RACHMANINOFF'S UNFINISHED STRING QUARTET

On a subsequent visit to Moscow, I found a copy of Rachmaninoff's unfinished string quartet among the secondhand offerings in a music shop. This acquisition proved to be helpful in 1990. The family of Andrei Sakharov requested that the slow movement from Rachmaninoff's string quartet be played at the memorial service for Sakharov held by the International League for Human Rights. A casual research revealed that the New York Public Library possessed the only readily available copy.

The following is an account reported in *The Washington Post* on January 5, 1990:

Members of the Lebenspiel Quartet then asked the New York Public Library for access to its copy of the two movements of the work known to exist, but the library would not let the music out, even for copying. Its manuscript, acquired when the piece's existence became known a few years ago, is very fragile.

Then Philip Kates, Philadelphia Orchestra violinist who leads the quartet, mentioned the dilemma to Dr. F. William Sunderman, a well–known Philadelphia pathologist and outstanding chamber music violinist. Sunderman dug into his world–renowned stack of chamber music.

"In his casual way, he called back and said, 'I have it and shall be pleased to present you with a copy'," said Marianne Brown, a Philadelphia lawyer and violinist who was involved with the planning of the memorial service.

Первый неоконченный квартет   First Quartet

С. РАХМАНИНОВ

SERGE RACHMANINOFF

II

РОМАНС   ROMANCE

First page of the score of the Rachmaninoff quartet.

84

Apparently this account also appeared in the *London Times*. I received a note from Dr. John Bateman, a scientist–pianist and friend living in London, stating, "Cheers! Congratulations on your victory over the New York Library."

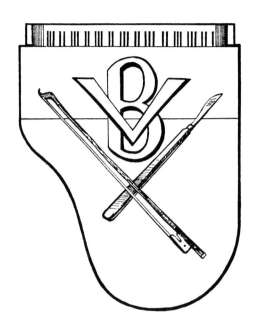

F. William Sunderman

Clarence K. Bauder.   Stanley P. Reimann

Ruus S. Bobes.   Thaddeus Rich

Adolph Vogel

Billroth Verein.

THE BILLROTH VEREIN

It is not unusual to find among physicians persons of musical achievements. From Phoebus–Apollo, the mythological god of medicine and music, to Helmholtz and Borodin, many examples could be cited of a successful fusing of art and science.

The glowing accounts of the musical soirees held in Dr. Theodore Billroth's home in Vienna during the past century, in which brilliant musicians including Joachim and Brahms were always present, inspired me to found a similar group in Philadelphia during the late 1930s. This group, which became known as the "Billroth Verein", met regularly on the first Sunday of every month for more than twenty–five years to play chamber music. The founding members included:

Violinists: *Thaddeus Rich*, Concertmaster and Assistant Conductor of the Philadelphia Orchestra.
F. William Sunderman, M.D., Clinical Professor of Medicine and Director of the Division of Metabolic Research, Jefferson Medical College.

Violists: *Samuel Laciar*, Music Critic, *Philadelphia Public Ledger*.
Samuel Rosen, Violist, Philadelphia Orchestra.

Cellists: *Adolph Vogel*, Former Cellist of the Philadelphia Orchestra and Music Publisher (Elkan–Vogel Co.).

Pianists: *Clarence K. Bawden*, Concert Pianist.
Russell D. Boles, M.D., Gastroenterologist affiliated with Philadelphia General and University of Pennsylvania Hospitals.
Stanley P. Reimann, M.D., Director of Laboratories, Lankenau Hospital and Founder and First Director of the Institute for Cancer Research.

Joseph Barrone, a columnist for the *Main Line Times*, wrote a feature article about the Billroth Verein. The article was published in this paper on April 9, 1953. The following is an excerpt taken from the account:

A few weeks ago, we were accorded the privilege of attending one of these musical sessions held at Dr. Boles' beautiful home in Penn Valley, and it was a memorable experience to listen to this small coterie of highly cultivated individuals, each a specialist in his own field, playing the great ennobling works of the old masters. There was good–natured comradeship, to be sure, but the playing was polished and purposeful at all times.

Here, indeed, were truly civilized men with a close spiritual kinship to the Renaissance and Classical eras, and as we came away from the extremely exhilarating evening, we could not help but recall Robert Schumann's significant words:

"In every age there are kindred souls. You who are of this fellowship, see that you weld the circle firmly, so that the truth of Art may shine ever more and more clearly, shedding joy and blessing far and near."

Chamber Music Notes

TRIO
(D-moll.)

I.

Violino.

A. ARENSKY, Op. 32.

Violin I – Arensky, *Opus 32.*

ANTON STEPANOVICH ARENSKY (1861–1906)

Opus 32   Trio in D Minor

I.   *Allegro Moderato*
II. *Scherzo Allegro Molto*
III. *Elegia Adagio*
IV. *Finale. Allegro non troppo*

Arensky inherited musical talents from both parents. His father was a physician and an excellent amateur cellist, and his mother was an accomplished pianist. He received his musical education at the St. Petersburg Conservatoire, majoring in theory and harmony, first with Zikke and later (1879–1882) with Rimsky–Korsakoff. After graduating from the St. Petersburg Conservatoire with honors, he was invited to assume the post as professor of harmony and counterpoint at the Moscow Conservatory under the directorship of Tanieff. This professorial position was a flattering acknowledgment of the confidence placed in Arensky's ability, since he was only 21 years of age at the time of his appointment. During his tenure at the Moscow Conservatory, Arensky taught and inspired a number of students, – including Sergei Rachmaninoff, who later became world famous. Arensky remained at the Moscow Conservatory until 1895 when he returned to St. Petersburg as the Director of Music at the Imperial Court Chapel.

During his Moscow days, Arensky became a member of the influential *New Circle of Five* whose objects were to continue the goals of the original *Circle of Five* (the

Kouchka[1]) in the furtherance of Russian classical music. With the passing of Moussorgsky (1881) and Borodin (1887), the original *Circle of Five* became inactive, and the *New Circle* took over their established responsibilities. Members of the *New Circle of Five* included Arensky, Liadov, Glazunov, Ippolitov–Ivanov, and Blumenfeld. These men met every Friday evening at the home of Balaief[2], their philanthropic sponsor, to deliberate and to play and listen to new Russian musical compositions. Balaief encouraged the men to write chamber music and made it a practice to "christen" every new work with champagne. Unlike the original *Circle* whose members strongly advocated the interjection of nationalism into the Russian musical idiom, the *New Circle* emphasized a more cosmopolitan approach and were greatly influenced by Tchaikovsky and his music. It is said that Tchaikovsky occasionally met with the group and encouraged them in their efforts.

The *D Minor Piano Trio* is the first of two trios that Arensky composed and is probably the most popular of his chamber music compositions. The trio was written in 1894 and is dedicated to the memory of Charles Davidoff

---

[1]The original *Circle of Five* was composed of five men of science: Borodin, a physician and chemist; Rimsky–Korsakoff, a naval officer; Cui, a professor of fortifications; Balakirev, a mathematician; and Moussorgsky, a military officer.

[2]Metrofan Balaief, a wealthy timber merchant, music publisher, and philanthropist, was an amateur viola player who was passionately fond of chamber music. In addition to sponsoring the activities of the *New Circle of Five*, Balaief provided symphonic concerts for the exclusive benefit of Russian composers.

(1838–1889), the world–famous German–Russian cellist whose first career was spent as a professor in the Conservatorium in Leipzig and his second in the Conservatoire in St. Petersburg.

The *D Minor Trio* unquestionably bears the hallmarks of Tchaikovsky's influence. It is an elegant, sensuous, and beautifully polished work of art. The opening movement is in *sonata* form. The violin introduces the lyrical first theme which, after 12 bars, is repeated by the cello. The second theme, *piu allegro*, is a lovely melody which follows in due course. Both themes are fully elaborated until the movement is closed with a graceful *coda, Adagio*.

The *Scherzo* is a sprightly, cheerful "Arensky Waltz" characterized by sweeping, virtuosic scalewise passages for the piano. The movement sparkles like diamonds in the sun.

The third movement is an *elegia* with muted strings as if in portrayal of mourning. The lyrical dialogues among the three voices are breath–takingly beautiful.

The *Finale* presents a dramatization of themes from the first movement and the *elegia*. It is a brilliant and effective ending to a remarkably graceful and romantic composition.

ANTON STEPANOVICH ARENSKY
Born: August 11, 1861, Novgorod, Russia.
Died: February 25, 1906, Terioki, Finland.

ANTON STEPANOVICH ARENSKY
Opus 35   Quartet No. 2 in A Minor

I.   *Moderato*
II. *Theme and Variations*
III. *FINALE, Andante sostenuto; Allegro moderato*

After Tchaikovsky's death in 1893, a number of his musical colleagues and disciplines wrote elegiac compositions honoring his memory. Arensky, a devoted disciple, made his contribution to Tchaikovsky's memory by composing a string quartet in which the focal point is the second movement. This movement comprises a set of seven variations based on the theme of one of Tchaikovsky's most enchantingly beautiful songs for children[1] entitled *Legend* and subtitled *Child Jesus Made a Garden.*

Arensky's second quartet was originally composed for two violins and two cellos; however, Arensky soon found this arrangement to be ineffective and impractical. As a consequence, he arranged the work for the conventional string quartet combination by substituting the viola for the first cello. The quartet consists of three movements.

The first movement is a mournful *dirge* in A Minor and portrays a feeling of sincere sadness. The second movement consists of a set of seven variations to Tchaikovsky's sensuous melody. The variations charmingly mirror the admiration that Arensky held for Tchaikovsky's music. The

---

[1]Tchaikovsky wrote sixteen songs for children in his *Opus 54.* Arensky's variations on Tchaikovsky's beautiful song, *Legend*, have been transcribed for string orchestra and will be readily recognized by symphony concert–goers.

last variation strongly reflects the *Andante Cantabile* of the second movement of Tchaikovsky's first string quartet (*Opus 11 in D Major*) and is, in my opinion, the most graceful and elegant of the variations. Arensky followed precedent by using the monumental ecclesiastical masterpiece, *Gloria in Excelsis Deo*, as the basic theme for the *Finale* movement. This same theme has been used by a number of composers: Beethoven used it(*theme Russe*) in the third movement of his eighth string quartet, *Opus 59, No. 2*; Moussorgsky, in the great chorus in the first act of *Boris Godounov*; and Rimsky–Korsakoff, in *The Tsar's Bride*.

Arensky's contributions to music were primarily those of a distinguished teacher of musical theory and composition and, secondarily, as a composer. Arensky did not leave a great number of instrumental compositions, but what he did leave have weight and command respect. Outstanding examples of his chamber music are his *Pianoforte Trio in D Minor (Opus 32)* dedicated to the memory of the virtuoso cellist, Karl Davidov, and his *Pianoforte Trio in D Major (Opus 51)*. Most of Arensky's chamber music clearly bears the impression of Tchaikovsky's influence.

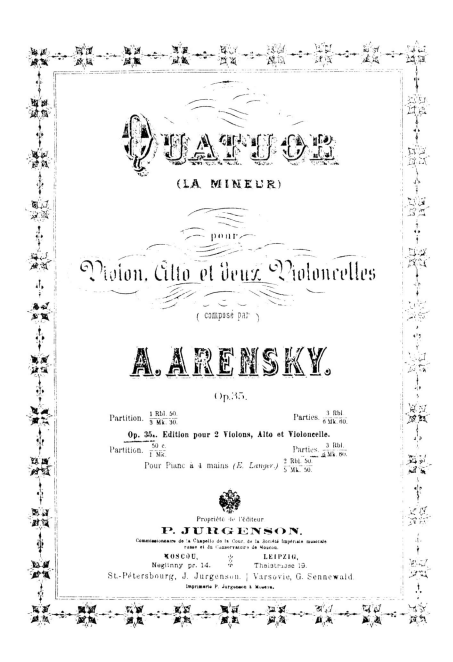

Cover from the *Opus 35* quartet of Arensky.

Tres Cuartetos

PARA

DOS VIOLINES, VIOLA Y VIOLONCELLO

Dedicados à su Padre

y compuestos
POR

J. C. DE ARRIAGA.

UNION MUSICAL ESPAÑOLA

EDITORES

MADRID

Cover from the *Three Quartets* of Arriaga.

JUAN CRISOSTOMO DE ARRIAGA(1806–1826)

Number 2   Quartet in A Major

I.   *Allegro con brio*
II. *Andante con variazioni*
III. *Menuetto*
IV. *Allegro*

Juan Crisostomo de Arriaga was born in Bilboa, Spain, in 1806 and died in Marseilles, France, in 1826, His exceptionally promising career was cut short by death from tuberculosis. As a child, Arriaga was recognized as a musical prodigy and was sent to the Paris Conservatory at the age of fifteen to study violin with Baillot and harmony and composition with Fetis. Under the skillful tutelage of his teacher, his talents for composition progressed rapidly. Arriaga did not leave many compositions, but those that he did leave have weight and are universally acknowledged to be masterpieces.

The first movement of the *Second Quartet* is written in *sonata* form in which the melodic line of all four instruments is distributed relatively equally. Although the first violin plays the leading roll, the melodic interest is given to the other three instruments. The second or slow movement consists of a majestic theme with five magnificent variations. The first variation, led by the first violin, contains beautifully ornamented configurations. The second violin and the cello take the lead in the second variation. The third variation is a doleful melody in a minor key played by the viola. The fourth variation is a *pizzicato* arrangement for all four instruments. The first violin returns to take the lead for the fifth (and last) variation.

99

The third movement is a sprightly *minuet*. The fourth movement contains an *Andante* followed by *Rondo* dance themes.

The quartets of Arriaga are characterized by their fresh, youthful purity and elegance of style. The musical world lost much with the premature death of this genius.

JUAN CRISOSTOMO DE ARRIAGA
Born: January 27, 1806, Bilbao, Spain.
Died: February, 1826, Marseilles, France.

2ᵉ QUATUOR.

Violino I.

ARRIAGA.

2392

Violin I – Arriaga, *Quartet No. 2.*

101

QUARTET

I.

Score – Bartók, *Opus 7.*

BÉLA BARTÓK (1881–1945)

Opus 7 Quartet No. 1

I. *Lento*
II. *Allegretto*
III. *Allegro vivace*

Bartók's contributions to music have gradually become accepted in the almost half century since his death; however, this acceptance has taken many years for attainment. Zoltán Kodály, composer, Hungarian compatriot, and friend of Bartók, comments:

> In the last fifty years, many people have tried to write new music – but few were able to cast it into lasting form. Bartók was one of the few – – though there are many who, sticking to the old and accustomed, do not like to listen to the voice of the new.

A synopsis of Bartók's early life is given in a *curriculum vitae* which he prepared at the age of 24.

December 1905
My biographical data are as follows: B. 1881. Nagyszentmiklós. At 7, lost my father; my mother (*née* Paula Voit) brought me up under very difficult conditions.

Aged 10, Nagyszolos; Mr. Altdörfer discovered my talent. First my mother taught me, then László Erkel in Pozsony, then I went on to the Budapest Academy of Music (Thomán, Koessler). My *Kossuth* symphony was performed and warmly acclaimed in Budapest in 1904; and later, in Manchester. In March this year, in Budapest, I scored a success as a pianist; also 2 weeks ago, in Manchester. A week ago my orchestral suite, in all its Hungarianness, caused a sensation <u>in Vienna</u>.

In 1907, Bartók was appointed professor of pianoforte at the Royal Hungarian Musical Academy in Budapest. He retired from this post in 1912 in order to devote his time entirely to composition and the study of Hungarian folk music. Based on his researches of old peasant folk songs, Bartók developed a new style of musical expression to which he adhered throughout his life. In 1920, it became necessary for him to earn his living by giving piano recitals in Europe, Great Britain, and the United States. For the next score of years, he oscillated between composing music and concertizing. In 1940, Bartók came to the United States to engage in a long concert tour. However, this tour had to be curtailed owing to his protracted illness from leukemia and tuberculosis. Bartók remained in this country throughout his illness and died in New York City on September 26, 1945.

Like Beethoven, Bartók's string quartets are his most representative works. It has been alleged that Bartók conceived his six string quartets as extensions of the last six quartets of Beethoven. And indeed, there are similarities. However, let it be quickly noted that Bartók's individual style of musical expression sets his compositions apart from those of all other composers. Perhaps it is the contrapuntal freedom and the latitude given each voice that elicit a comparison of Bartók's quartets to those of late Beethoven.

Bartók's first quartet was completed in 1909 and went unplayed for two years. None of the professional quartets at that time was willing to play the composition publicly. However, four Budapest friends decided to take matters into their own hands by forming a new quartet to play Bartók. For many years, this group, which became known as the Hungarian Quartet, was the only outlet that Bartók had. Bartók paid his indebtedness to the group by dedicating the second quartet to "Au Quator Hongrois Waldbauer, Temesvary, Kornstein, Kerpely." The Hungarian Quartet maintained its identity until 1945.

Bartók's first quartet opens with a slow *fugue* reminiscent of the opening movement of the *C Sharp Minor Quartet* of Beethoven (*Opus 131*). At about the halfway point, a new section begins in which the cello carries the melody. This subsides with a quiet recapitulation of the opening *fugue* an octave higher. The second movement follows (*attacca*) without interruption from a gradual *accelerando* to *Allegretto*. The transition leads to a second theme which is interrupted by a rhythmic *fugue*. The third movement proves to be a high–spirited, capricious, and refulgent *Finale*.

BÉLA BARTÓK

Born: March 25, 1881, Nagyszentmiklós, Hungary (now Rumania).
Died: September 26, 1945, New York, New York, U.S.A.

BÉLA BARTÓK

Opus 114   Quartet No. 6

I.   *Mesto, Vivace*
II.   *Mesto, Marcia*
III. *Mesto, Burletta*
IV. *Mesto*

Béla Bartók, the eminent Hungarian composer, pianist, and musicologist, is one of the gigantic contributors to the musical culture of the twentieth century. His father was the director of an agricultural institute in Budapest, and his mother, Paula, was a highly respected pianist and teacher. Paula Bartók began teaching her son to play the piano at the age of five. It was through her devotion and encouragement that he began to improvise folk music on the piano at the age of nine. At the age of 13, he arranged a composition (*The Course of the Danube*) for violin and piano.

Bartók's six string quartets date from 1907 to 1939 and cover the major portion of his creative career. The sixth quartet was written in the autumn of 1939 and was the last composition that he wrote in his native land.

The sixth quartet had originally been commissioned by Zoltán Szekely for the New Hungarian Quartet. However, owing to the outbreak of World War II and Bartók's emigration to the United States, contact with Szekely was lost. Subsequently, the sixth quartet was dedicated to the Kolisch Quartet, who gave its first performance in New York on January 20, 1941.

Bartók left Budapest and arrived in New York on April 11, 1940 and on April 13 gave his first concert at the

Coolidge Festival in Washington in collaboration with his compatriot, the Hungarian violinist, Szigeti. It is noteworthy that soon after coming to the United States, Bartók received an excellent offer from Randall Thompson, at that time director of The Curtis Institute of Music, to teach composition at The Institute. Considering the hardships that Bartók encountered during the remaining five years of his life, it is regrettable that he declined this prestigious offer.

The structure of the sixth quartet deviates markedly from the usual quartet form. Each movement begins with the same motto–theme which provides a unifying element for the entire quartet. In the first movement, the theme is announced by a viola soliloquy. The basic idiom is then used as an introduction to the *Marcia* with the two violins and viola playing in unison and the cello carrying the theme. The *Marcia* is a strange type of march which is faintly suggestive of the *Alla Marcia* in Beethoven's A Minor quartet, *Opus 132*. It is noteworthy that Bartók employed slow, heavy *glissandos* in the *Marcia* section to produce weird sounds. In the third movement, a burlesque (*Burletta*) is inserted after the motto–theme introduction. In this movement, the violins are directed at certain places to play notes a quarter of a tone lower. At other places, it is specified to play "a strong *pizzicato* so that the string rebounds off the fingerboard." The last movement is profoundly pessimistic. In the slow finale, marked *Mesto*, the melody of sadness gives the gesture of a tragic farewell.

Dedicated to the Kolisch Quartet

SIXTH STRING QUARTET

1st Violin

I

BÉLA BARTOK

B & H 9103

Sole Selling Agents: **Boosey & Hawkes, Ltd.,** 295 Regent Street, London, W.1
All Rights Reserved   *Paris · Bonn · Capetown · Sydney · Toronto · Buenos Aires · New York*   Printed in England

Violin I – Bartok, *Opus 114.*

LUDWIG VON BEETHOVEN
Born: December 16, 1770, Bonn, Germany.
Died: March 26, 1827, Vienna, Austria.

LUDWIG VON BEETHOVEN

Opus 18, No. 1   Quartet in F Major

I. *Allegro*
II. *Adagio affettuoso ed appassionato*
III. *Scherzo, Allegro molto*
IV. *Allegro*

The six quartets that comprise *Opus 18* were written between 1798 and 1800 and were published by Mollo in Vienna in 1801. The *F Major Quartet* was completed by June 25, 1799, on which day Beethoven gave a copy of the manuscript to his loyal friend, Amenda, "in remembrance of our friendship." Amenda, a Latvian theological student, violinist, and tutor for Prince Lobkowitz's children was obliged to return to Latvia. Later, on July 1, 1801, Beethoven wrote to Amenda not to lend the manuscript to anyone since the quartet had been revised. It would thus appear that the final version of the quartet had not been completed until just prior to publication.

The first known performance of the quartet took place in December, 1880 at the apartment of Count and Countess Deym. Afterwards, the Countess wrote to her sister:

> Beethoven, that real angel, permitted us to hear his new quartets, which have not yet been engraved. . . you can imagine what a treat it was for us.

These historical notes will serve to authenticate the time relationships for the *F Major Quartet*.

The numerical order of the six quartets of *Opus 18* does not represent their chronological order of composition. From quotations in Beethoven's sketch–books, it has been deduced that the quartets were composed in the order of 3, 1, 2, 5, with uncertainty about the placements of quartets 4 and 6. On the advice of Ignaz Schuppanzigh,[1] Beethoven wisely decided to place the *F Major Quartet* first instead of the less impressive *D Major Quartet (No. 3)*, which had been composed earlier. The order of the grouping was objective without pretense of any relationship of one quartet to another.

The first movement of the *F Major Quartet*, *Allegro con brio*, is a striking example of Beethoven's genius in "working" a brief motif relentlessly into the creation of a remarkable expansive masterpiece. The motif consists of only six notes. This group of six notes appears 102 times in

in the 303 measures contained in the first movement. The motif is treated not only as primary and secondary melodies but also becomes woven into the web of counterpoint.

Needless to note that the motif of the first movement underwent many laborious permutations and transformations before it reached the ultimate form that

---

1Schuppanzigh was the leader of a quartet in which Prince Carl Licknowsky played second violin; Weiss, viola; and Kraft, cello. This group met regularly at Prince Licknowsky's home with Beethoven frequently in attendance. In 1808, Schuppanzigh became the first violinist of the Rasoumovsky Quartet with Count Andreas Rasoumovsky, a Russian nobleman, playing second violin. The Rasoumovsky Quartet rehearsed weekly for several years with Beethoven serving as their coach. Beethoven dedicated the three quartets of *Opus 59* to Count Rasoumovsky.

was acceptable to Beethoven. Two of his sketch–books contain a total of sixteen pages of changes and experimental arrangements. In the illustration are shown two discarded examples in which the motif was composed in 4/4, not 3/4 meter.

The *Adagio affettuoso ed appassionato* movement in D Minor is a somber, melodious movement of exceptional depth of feeling. In composing the movement, it is alleged that Beethoven pictured the parting of two lovers and "the scene in the burial vault of Shakespeare's *Romeo and Juliet*.[2] The slow movements of *Opus 59, No. 1* and *Opus 74* bear similar tragic imports; the second movement of *Opus 18, No. 1* is undoubtedly their precursors.

The *Scherzo* offers a mild release from the depressed, heavy–hearted mood of the preceding movement. The movement is colorful and leaps from *pianissimos* through *sforzandos* and *crescendos* into the trio. The trio fluctuates between octaves, *arpeggios*, and modified scale passages to return to the recapitulation.

The *Finale* is a pleasing, vigorous movement, although it is the least euphuistic and sophisticated of the four.

---

[2]In the unused sketch for the *Adagio* movement, Beethoven wrote *les derniers soupirs* (the last breaths), which would tend to support the veracity of this anecdote.

Beethoven Out Walking (c. 1820).
Pencil drawing by Josef Daniel Bohm (1794–1865).

LUDWIG VON BEETHOVEN (1770–1827)

Opus 18, No. 4   **Quartet in C Minor**

I.   *Allegro ma non tanto*
II.   *SCHERZO. Andante scherzoso quasi Allegretto*
III.   *MENUETTO. Allegretto*
IV.   *Allegro*

Most authorities concur in the opinion that the six quartets comprising *Opus 18* were written between 1798 and 1800; however, a few scholars, such as Sir George Groves, place these compositions somewhat earlier since extant sketches go back to Beethoven's fledgling days in Bonn. As in the case of most composers, thematic material is collected over a period of years and then incorporated into a composition. It seems unlikely, however, that the *Opus 18* quartets were written before 1795. In that year, Count Apponyi offered Beethoven a commission to write a string quartet. Beethoven declined since he felt he had not attained sufficient maturity to engage in such a serious undertaking. Be that as it may, the six quartets of *Opus 18* were published in two volumes in 1801 by the Mollo Press in Vienna with the dedication to Prince Lobkowitz, one of Beethoven's firm friends and admirers.

It has been established that the numerical designation of the quartets of *Opus 18* is not in their order of composition. It seems probable that the *C Minor Quartet* was composed last. The original handwritten copy of the six quartets was lost and has never been located. As a consequence, the chronology of the quartets has been a matter of conjecture and speculation.

The first movement, *Allegro ma non tanto*, begins with a soft, beautiful, passionate melody which terminates abruptly at measure 13 with a dramatic burst of loud, alternate tonic and dominant chords followed by an emotional recapitulation. The *fortissimo* chords are repeated elsewhere in the movement and represent a marked deviation in composition from the classical forms of Haydn and Mozart. The movement is highly imaginative and "throbs with joyous fervor."

The second movement, *Andante scherzoso*, is in marked contrast to the profound previous movement. Beethoven developed the movement as a cannon. It is witty and has a pleasantly rhythmic design.

The *Menuetto* opens with similar notes and motif as the *Allegro* and thus imparts a sense of unity to the composition. The alternating *forzandos* are reminiscent of Mozart's device of accenting weak and strong beats in the *Menuetto* movement of the *G Major Quartet* (*K. 387*). The trio in A Flat is a magnificent, simple theme first carried by the second violin and then by the viola and cello and ornamented by the first violin playing in triplets. At the *del cappo*, Beethoven wrote, "*la seconda volta si prenda il tempo piu Allegro.*" The return tempo is usually taken at about twice the original speed. This faster tempo imparts a frenzied excitement for the closing statement.

The fourth movement, *Allegro*, is of heroic stature. Helm[1] gives the following metaphoric description for the movement:

---

[1]Helm, T.: *Beethoven's Streichquartette*.

One imagines four combatants battling against each other, clad in shining armour, armed with sword and shield. At the outset, the first violin, the *primus inter pares* among the knightly company, is alone in the arena, a young hero trying his strength with supple limb and sinew; but soon the three other champions enter the lists and the jousting commences. (Notice the exquisite imitations in the third section.) There is a momentary halt, and in the musical interlude (first in A Flat, then in C) one seems to see on the rostrum wreathed with flowery garlands a glimpse of a lovely lady waving encouragement and signalling her favours.

The *C Minor Quartet* is undoubtedly the most sophisticated and polished of the quartets in the *Opus 18* series. It portends to the great works of Beethoven's second and third periods. It is noteworthy that all of the movements in *Opus 18, Number 4*, are in the same key, – either C Minor or C Major, and that the trio of the *minuet* alone departs.

FRANZ JOSEPH MAX PRINCE LOBKOWITZ (1772–1816)
Stippled engraving by C. H. Pfeiffer after F. A. Oelenhainz.

LUDWIG VON BEETHOVEN   (1770–1827)

Opus 18, Number 6   Quartet in B Major

I.   *Allegro con brio*
II.   *Adagio ma non troppo*
III. *Scherzo – allegro*
IV.   *La Malinconia – adagio*
      Allegretto quasi allegro

The original handwritten copies of Beethoven's first six quartets have disappeared. As a consequence, most of the speculations regarding the chronology of the quartets have been elicited from Beethoven's sketchbooks.[1] It is apparent that repeated revisions were made in all of the quartets before they were published in two installments in June and October of 1801 under the title: *"Six Quatuors pour deux Violons, Alto et Violoncelle,* compose et dedie a Son Altesse Monseigneur le Prince Regnant de Lobkowitz par Louis van Beethoven. (Euvre 18. 1er Livraison a Vienne chez T. Mollo et Comp. (Edition No. 159)."

Although the precise dates of the composition of the *Opus 18* quartets cannot be ascertained with certainty, nevertheless, it seems probable that they were written between 1798 and 1800. It is known that the chronological order in which the quartets were composed does not correspond to their numerical designation. It is surmised the *Opus 18, Number 6* was perhaps the fifth, in chronologic succession.

---

[1]Beethoven went nowhere without his sketchbooks, – a characteristic which distinguished him from most of the other composers.

The opening theme in the first movement of the *Opus 18, Number 6* quartet is easygoing, happy, and relaxing. The movement consists of a theme in the key of B flat major of simple, diatonic harmony followed by a brief melancholy second theme in the minor key. The movement concludes with a re–exposition of the opening section.

The slow movement (*Adagio*) is a graceful melody with ornamentation which is initially played by the first violin alone and is then unrolled in rich, ingenious counterpoint by the other three instruments. It has been said that this movement must have been composed in one of the rare, serene moments in Beethoven's life.

The *Scherzo* is a witty, imaginative, and boisterous movement which has been designated as the first piece of jazz that was ever composed. The rhythmic vigor is the movement's most salient feature.

The *Adagio* in the *Finale* carries the inscription *La Malinconia* with a subtitle in Italian (see example) which

translated states, "This movement must be played with the greatest refinement." After a pause, the *Malinconia* section gives way to a lively *Allegretto quasi allegro* in the manner of a country dance. The introspective melancholic theme returns for brief periods, and the movement finally ends in a wild *Prestissimo* which seems to signify Beethoven's triumph over melancholic despair.

ANDREAS KYRILLOVITCH RASUMOVSKY (1752–1836)
Oil painting by J. B. Lampi.

LUDWIG VON BEETHOVEN   (1770–1827)

Opus 59, No. 1   Quartet in F Major

Quartet number 7, completed in 1806

I.   *Allegro*
II.   *Allegretto vivace e sempre scherzando*
III. *Adagio molto e mesto*
IV. *Theme Russe*

The seventeen Beethoven quartets are usually divided into three periods:

The first period includes the six quartets of *Opus 18* in which the youthful Beethoven followed the tradition of the earlier masters, – notably Haydn and Mozart.

The second period includes the three Rasoumovsky quartets (*Opus 59*), the Harp quartet (*Opus 74*), and the Serioso (*Opus 95*) in which Beethoven relied on his own mastery of composition.

The third period, known as the Period of Reflection, includes *Opus 127, 130, 131, 132, 133*, and *135* (his last composition).

After completing the *Opus 18* quartets in 1801, Beethoven did not resume quartet writing until 1806. He was stimulated to return to this medium of musical expression by Count Rasoumovsky, the Russian Ambassador in Vienna and a well–known amateur violinist. Unlike Archduke Rudolph and Prince Lobkowitz, Rasoumovsky was not a major benefactor of Beethoven. Not much is known about Rasoumovsky's commission excepting that he expressed the wish that Russian folk songs be incorporated into the quartets. Beethoven completed the quartets during the late summer months of that year. In compliance with Rasoumovsky's wish, Beethoven incorporated Russian themes into the first and second quartet[1] but omitted them in the third.

At the outset, the *Opus 59* quartets were not received favorably by the musical fraternity in Vienna. They were played privately from manuscript on several occasions during 1807. Clementi, a virtuoso pianist of the period, is said to have asked Beethoven, "Surely you do not consider these works to be music?" Beethoven replied, "They are not for you, but for a later age."

Beethoven had offered the publishing rights to the *Opus 59* quartets to Breitkopf and Hartel of Leipzig on November 18, 1806 for 600 florins, but this offer was declined. The quartets were finally published in January 1808 by Schreivogel.

Over the ensuing years, the *Opus 59* quartets gained universal recognition and acclaim. In 1831, the three quartets were played in Paris by the Bohrer Quartet and were given an enthusiastic reception. The next year, the *finale* of the third quartet was played by the entire string section of the Paris Conservatory Orchestra with prodigious effectiveness. Similar spirited performances of this movement were given by the Vienna Philharmonic Orchestra.

It would seem appropriate at this juncture to recount a few interesting items about Rasoumovsky who

---

[1]*Theme–Russe* in the *Finale, Opus 59, No. 1* and the popular *Gloria in Excelsis Deo* in the *Allegretto* movement of *Opus 59, No. 2*.

commissioned Beethoven to compose *Opus 59*, since his name is inseparably attached to the quartets. Two brothers, named Razum and differing in age by nineteen years, became singers in the choir of the Russian Court. The brothers came from peasant Cossack stock in the Ukraine. Both men rose into positions of political prominence and great wealth which, according to Thayer, was due "to the gratifications of lascivious lusts of two imperial princesses" who later became Empress Elizabeth Petrovna (1709–1762) and Catherine II (1729–1796).[2] These noble ladies not only provided their paramours with the titles of Counts Rasoumovsky[3] but also selected their wives from families of the nobility. The patronage of the Empresses even extended to the children of the two Counts.

The Rasoumovsky of *Opus 59* fame was Andreus Kyrillovich, the fourth son of the younger Count Rasoumovsky. His mother was said to have been a Ukranian peasant, although it is conjectured that she may actually have been Catherine the Great. Andreus received naval training in his youth and was elevated to the rank of naval captain at the age of twenty–five and then was transferred to the diplomatic corps. He held ambassadorial posts in several European cities, and, according to Thayer, was :

less famous for his diplomacy than notorious for the profuseness of his expenditures and for his amours with women of the highest rank, the Queen of Naples, not excepted.

---

[2]Also called Catherine the Great. She was Empress from 1762 to 1796.

[3]The older brother was the paramour of Elizabeth; the younger, of Catherine.

True to the traditions of the Razum family, Count Andreus Rasoumovsky became a musician and excelled as a violinist. In 1808, he served on occasion as the second violinist in the Schuppanzigh Quartet, Vienna's leading quartet, which Beethoven coached.

In 1815, Count Rasoumovsky was elevated to the rank of a Russian Prince. He lived lavishly in Vienna in a grandiose palace surrounded by a luxurious library and valuable objects of art. At the profusely extravagant receptions which the Prince tendered visiting monarchs, Beethoven was always included in the guest list. Unfortunately, Rasoumovsky's palace was destroyed by fire soon after he had attained his princehood. The ruling Russian emperor, Alexander I (1777–1825), loaned Rasoumovsky 400,000 silver rubles to defray the cost of reconstruction. Unfortunately, this amount proved to be insufficient to restore the property, and the Prince was obliged to relinquish the ownership. With this loss, Prince Rasoumovsky faded out of the history of Vienna; however, his name achieved immortality by association with the *Opus 59* quartets.

The Rasoumovsky quartets (*Opus 59*) serve as the link between the first and second periods of the Beethoven quartets. The movements of the seventh quartet are structurally in sonata form. The first movement, *Allegro*, begins with the melody in the cello with the expansion of the theme by the first violin. Actually, the text of the entire movement is announced in the first four measures by the cello. A rich variety of ancillary material is introduced, and the development turns almost entirely on the initial theme.

The opening phrase is repeated at the end of the movement, and the movement terminates majestically.

The *Allegretto vivace* movement serves as a *scherzo*. The theme consists of several independent sections which, at first, do not appear to be interrelated but eventually become unified. The movement ends in a mysterious *pianissimo* which finally breaks into a brisk *fortissimo*.

The *Adagio* movement is a sad, mournful, sublime, and gentle lament. On the manuscript of this movement, Beethoven inscribed, "A weeping willow or acacia tree on my brother's grave." This movement is beautiful, profound, and tragic and is a tribute to the loss of his brother who died in infancy. In Cobbett's words, "Happy [are] the artists who can understand and interpret such a masterpiece!" A magnificent *cadenza* for the first violin and a trill at the end of the movement leads directly into the *finale*.

The *Allegro* (*Theme Russe*) is based upon the Russian song, *Akh! talan li moi, talan takoi* (Ah, my luck, such luck!). The movement is spirited, virile, and vigorous. At the end, it sinks into a slow *pianissimo* which culminates into a *fortissimo Presto*.

Some forty years ago in conversation with members of the then famous London String Quartet, Pennington, the first violinist, made a remark which has lingered in my memory. He remarked that after a vacation period when the members of the Quartet had not played together for a month or so, they invariably began their rehearsal with Beethoven *Opus 59, Number 1*. This quartet was not only their favorite but individually and collectively they felt that they had never completely mastered it.

Beethoven in His Study.
Painting by C. Schloesser.

LUDWIG VON BEETHOVEN (1770–1827)

Opus 59, No. 3 Quartet in C Major

Quartet number 9

I.   *Introduction Andante con moto. Allegro vivace*
II. *Andante con moto quasi Allegretto*
III. *Menuetto Grazioso*
IV. *Allegro molto*

Europeans refer to the third Rasoumovsky quartet as the *Eroica Quartet* by analogy to the *Third Symphony*. In mood, rhythm, and structure, this quartet stands in marked contrast to the first and second quartets of *Opus 59*.

Of the three quartets of *Opus 59*, the third in the set was much better received when it first appeared than the first two quartets. It was obviously more appealing owing to the melodic and symphonic character and to its similarity in structure to the *Opus 18* quartets. It is conjectured that Beethoven's return to the earlier style was probably stimulated by Rasoumovsky, to whom the *Opus 59* quartets were dedicated. According to Altman:

> The third page of the cover in Riedl's edition (probably the first) bears the Rasoumovsky coat of arms with the motto: *Famam extendere factis* (to spread abroad his fame through deeds [*Virgil*]).

The *Introduction* of 29 measures is clouded in an atmosphere of mystery and and holds the listener in suspense with wandering harmonies that finally are resolved by moving the viola A Flat to to an all important G in the measure before the *Allegro*. The mysterious clouds then disappear, and the music becomes firmly resolved in an *Allegro* in the key of C Major.

129

The *Introduction* is followed by a sprightly melodious recitative played by the first violin and then by a vigorous contrasting restatement by all four voices. This movement is capricious and whimsical throughout the mainbody and ends *stringendo* in a chromatic scale climaxed by two *fortissimo* chords.

The second movement, *Andante con moto*, begins with the cello playing a *pizzicato* organ point over a haunting, pulsating, and slightly monotonous melody. A number of analysts have pointed out that the first two sections suggest a song–form; the latter sections, however, have "no defined character, leaving the spirit to wander in a waste of vague melancholy." The mood of the movement is sad, soulful, and sincere.

The *Menuetto* movement, subtitled *Grazioso*, is written in *sonata* form in the manner of Haydn. The movement portrays a relaxed, charmingly graceful spirit. It concludes with a *Coda* that begins *pianissimo* and broadens into a *crescendo* that leads without pause into the *Finale*.

The last movement displays powerful, energetic, rhythmic forces over a counterpoint that creates a majestic type of exhilaration for the music. The movement is essentially a *fugue* and is recognized as one of the most monumental in the entire quartet literature. Beethoven may have written a more profound movement but certainly never one that was more triumphant.

LUDWIG VON BEETHOVEN   (1770–1827)

Opus 74   Quartet in E Flat Major
The Harp

I.   *Poco Adagio – Allegro*
II.   *Adagio ma non troppo*
III. *Presto – Piu presto quasi prestissimo*
IV. *Allegretto con Variazioni*

After completing the Rasoumovsky quartets in 1806, Beethoven did not compose in the quartet medium until 1809. The published version of the tenth quartet appeared in December 1810 under the following title: *"Quatour pour deux violins, viola et violoncelle,* compose et dedie a son Altesse le Prince regnant de Lobkowitz, Duc de Raudnitz, par L. V. Beethoven. Propriete des editeurs. OEuv. 74, a Leipzig chez Breitkopf et Hartel."

It was in the midst of "sorrow and tears" that Beethoven wrote the *Opus 74* Quartet. In 1809, the French army drove the Austrian army to the Danube and marched toward Vienna. The court fled the city and Beethoven found himself almost penniless without the financial assistance of his imperial patron, Prince Regent Lobkowitz, and his imperial pupil, Archduke Rudolph.[1] Beethoven remained

---

[1]The piano sonata, *Opus 81a,* was written during the French invasion and dedicated to Archduke Rudolph, bearing the inscription *Lebewohl, Abwesenheit und Wiedersehn* (Farewell, Absence, and Return). Beethoven jotted a memorandum for the first movement. "The Farewell, Vienna, 4th May 1809, the date of departure of my honored Archduke, Prince Rudolph." Another memorandum was also written, apparently after the peace was signed, "The Return of my honored Archduke, Prince Rudolph, 30 January 1810."

in Vienna for the two months during which the city was under siege and when food was scarce and costly and the summer heat almost unbearable. In addition to these hardships, Beethoven suffered from tragic loneliness imposed upon him by his loss of hearing. *Opus 74* was composed under these adverse circumstances and, as a consequence, it has been said that the *Opus 74* Quartet is the "key to the soul of Beethoven.

Soon after its publication, *Opus 74* acquired the nickname *The Harp*. This naive title was bestowed because of the *pizzicato* passages in the first movement as well as the successively rolling passages by the cello, viola, and violins.

Many printing errors appeared in the original edition of *Opus 74*. Beethoven complained about these to the publisher, Breitkopf and Härtel, stating, "I have noticed that even the clearest writing is misconstrued." Regrettably, many of these printing errors still remain uncorrected and have led to frustrations in performance by both professional and amateur players. For example, in the Peters editions, the *Poco Adagio* in the first movement is wrongly marked C (*alla breve*). This section is correctly marked C (*i.e.*, 4/4 meter) in the Breitkopf and Härtel editions; however, in the same movement, Breitkopf and

Hartel left out the first repetition marks of the *Allegro* section, so that a novice would obviously make the repetition from the beginning of the movement.[2]

The introduction (*Poco Adagio*) of the first movement begins with hushed tones of a mysterious, melancholy motif of four notes. The motif proceeds *semper piano* as though

travelling through a long tunnel and then suddenly after a one bar crescendo bursts energetically into the *Allegro* section with its harp–like theme. Every note of the opening section gives the impression of being a tear.

Although all four instruments share equally in the main body of the *Allegro* section, nevertheless, in the coda the first violin is given a concerto–like solo assignment that calls for both technical and artistic virtuosity. This *furioso* passage provides a peroration for the movement. In the concluding measures of the first movement, Marliave notes, "Every bar seems charged with the vital force which has triumphed over the despair of the introductory *Adagio*, and dispelled its haunting melancholy."

The second movement (*Adagio*) is one of intense pathos and unrelieved sadness. It may be compared with the *Cavatina* movement of the great B Flat Quartet, *Opus 130*. Critics have accused Beethoven of being overly sentimental in this movement; as Marliave points out:

---

[2]A list of inaccuracies was compiled by Rontgen in 1862 and later by W. Altmann in 1911. The later corrections appear in the partitur of Edition Eulenburg.

If one were looking for traces of sentimentality in Beethoven's music one could perhaps find it in the slow movement of *Opus 74*, but of a quality so noble and sincere as to transcend criticism and to lift it out of all possibility of comparison with the false emotion and sentimental hypocrisy found so often in the works of Beethoven's successors, and even in Mendelssohn.

The *Scherzo* is a *presto* movement in C Minor combined with a *prestissimo* trio in C Major written in steady counterpoint successions. The trio section is repeated and is followed by a re–entry into the beginning *presto* section. The movement ends in a *pianissimo* and is marked *attacca il sequente, i.e.*, leading into the fourth movement without a break.

The finale (*Allegretto*) is a beautiful, simple melodious theme with a set of six noble variations. The variations are alternatively spirited and pensive. The second and fourth variations are especially noteworthy for their poetic inspiration. In the second variation, the viola takes over the cheerful, heartfelt melody to the fullest glorification of the instrument. In the fourth variation, the first violin is permitted to sing out the lush melody in sustained quarter notes to the soft accompaniment of the other instruments. The concluding figure in the movement is an *Allegro* preceded by a *Vivace – accelerando e crescendo poco a poco*. The final unison passage rises to a flaming *fortissimo* and then ends abruptly on two *piano* chords.

LUDWIG VON BEETHOVEN   (1770–1827)

Opus 95   Quartet in F Minor

Serioso   Quartet # 11

**Dedicated to Nikolaus Zmeskall von Domanovetz
Completed, October 1810
First performance, May 1814 in Vienna**

I.   *Allegro con brio*
II.   *Allegretto ma non troppo*
III. *Allegro assai vivace ma serioso*
IV.   *Larghetto – Allegretto agitato*

The autographed copy of *Opus 95* (which now reposes in the Imperial and Royal Library of Vienna) contains the following inscription: *"Quartett serioso* – 1810 – in the month of October. Dedicated to Herr von Zmeskall by his friend L v Bthvn and written in the month of October."

The date obviously relates to the completion of the composition, since certain sketches of the work have been found dated May 1810. The quartet was written during a period when Beethoven's serious intentions of marrying Theresa Malfatti had not materialized. It is surmised that his rejection in marriage may have been the reason for titling the composition *Serioso* and for the dedication to his intimate friend, Zmeskall, who was his confidante in the love affair.

The eleventh quartet (*Opus 95*) is the shortest of the sixteen quartets. It has sometimes been referred to as a transitional work, since it is the last of the middle series of quartets. Beethoven was already deaf when the quartet was written. The quartet is a drama of personal will against fate and obviously was written in an irritable and ill–tempered mood. Although the work had been completed in 1810, nevertheless, Beethoven withheld publication until 1816.

The first movement (*Allegro con brio*) begins with an angry outburst of eleven notes by the four voices playing in unison. This sudden eruption at once creates a troubled, turbulent atmosphere and imparts a seriousness not observed in preceding quartets. Out of this violent medium emerge melodic fragments in the key of D Flat. However, the angry motive continues to reassert itself, even in the diminuendo passage in the last eight bars of the movement.

The *Allegretto* movement becomes linked to the first movement by having the cello begin the movement with a partial transcription of the angry notes of the initial theme. The transposed linkage is shown in the figure. The entire

movement portrays a saddened, troubled spirit. Although it is written in the key of D Major, nevertheless, the movement is characterized by a restless shifting in key structure. After the insertion of an unexpected *arpeggio* for the violins, the movement ends quietly in its initial key. A sustained diminished seventh chord in the final bar precedes the sudden vigorous impetuosity of the third movement.

The *Allegro vivace* movement in 3/4 time replaces the usual *scherzo*. The third movement is built around two figures, as shown in the illustration. The galloping motion

produced by these two rhythms in all four parts creates an exhausting tension. The trio, even though bowed *legato*, does little to relieve the turbulence.

In the fourth movement, seven measures of a slow, grieving introduction precede the agitated *finale* in A Minor. Basil Lam observes that Beethoven found in the last movement a perfect conclusion for his *Serioso* quartet, – "too heartfelt for cynicism" and "too light . . . for the tense smile of the . . . stoic." To the writer, the movement displays Beethoven's fortitude in the face of adversity.

At the conclusion of the *finale*, Beethoven relieves the hypertensive environment by inserting a totally unexpected comic opera *coda*, as if to shrug his shoulders and say, "So what?"

Copy of the frontispiece of the original edition – Beethoven, *Opus 130*.
Ornamental title by A. Kurka.

LUDWIG VON BEETHOVEN   (1770–1827)

Opus 130   Quartet in B Flat Major

I.   *Adagio, ma non troppo – Allegro*
II.   *Presto*
III. *Andante con moto, ma non troppo*
IV. *Allegro assai (Alla danza tedesca)*
V.   *Cavatina (Adagio molto expressivo)*
VI. (Original) *Grosse Fuge, Opus 133 (B Flat Major)*
       Overtura; Allegro – Fuga: Allegro molto e con brio
VI. (Revision) *Finale Allegro*

David Martin, the eminent British violinist, teacher, and former leader of the BBC Quartet, told me many years ago that Beethoven's thirteenth quartet should always be referred to as the *"Great" B Flat*. For many of us, this quartet remains unsurpassed in the chamber music literature for its tremendous range of music expression from lighthearted wit to deep emotion. Beethoven acknowledged the *Great B Flat* quartet to be his favorite.

Near the end of 1825, Beethoven completed the *Great B Flat Major* string quartet, *Opus 130*. It was performed by the Schuppanzigh Quartet in Vienna on March 21, 1826. The quartet contained six movements, – the first five of which were met with immediate success. However, the sixth movement, labelled in the manuscript as *Overtura–Fuga*, had an adverse reaction.

At the earnest solicitation of the publisher Artaria, Beethoven consented with much reluctance to publish the sixth movement (*Grand Fugue*) separately and to compose a shorter movement as a replacement. After a waiting period of several months, Beethoven composed the *Finale Allegro* movement in November 1826 to replace the *Grand Fugue*. This replacement proved to be Beethoven's last manuscript.[1] The thirteenth quartet with the substituted *Finale Allegro* movement was published as *Opus 130* and dedicated to Prince Galitizin; the *Grand Fugue* was published separately as *Opus 133* and dedicated to Archduke Rudolph.

Beethoven's thirteenth quartet comprises six extraordinarily contrasting movements. The first movement, according to Cobbett, "appears to be a struggle between two instincts in the same individual: the gently imploring instinct and that of inexorable violence." Preceded by a slow introduction, an animated *Allegro* follows which consists of two themes, as illustrated.

Theme I

Theme II

Theme I bursts forth as an agitated, violent passage which is opposed by a powerful second theme (II). The forceful rhythm of theme II 𝅘𝅥 𝅘𝅥 𝅘𝅥𝅮 𝅘𝅥𝅮 𝅘𝅥. is emphatically reiterated at least eighteen times in the first movement.

The *Presto* (second movement) is actually a *Scherzo* although it was not so designated. The brevity, the color,

---

[1]Peters of Leipzig applied for the publication of the *B Flat Major Quartet* but stipulated that the manuscript must first be submitted for approval. Beethoven curtly refused Peters and gave the manuscript to Artaria of Vienna for publication.

the texture, and the striking rhythm unite to impart an ephemeral ballet atmosphere. The four parts are bound together in an architectural design in the finest string quartet tradition.

The third movement, an *Andante con moto* was called by Schumann an *intermezzo* by "reason of its depth of fantasy, its whimsical blending of conflicting melodies, . . . its ethereal yet firmly coherent construction built upon unified themes growing one out of another and making the movement a unique example of thematic variation." The movement has also been referred to as a sonata without development. The melodies are rich and of the highest order of beauty.

The notation for the fourth movement (*Alla danza tedesca*) means that this movement should be played in the style of a German waltz, i.e., quick. *Tedesca* is the Italian word for waltz. The melodies are gay and are in sharp contrast to those of the preceding third movement. The 1/16 rests in the first and third bars of the illustration call for

Alla danza tedesca

Allegro assai

brief waits which are frequently referred to by the German name of *Luftpause*. These *Luftpauses* permit the resonance of one phrase to die out before beginning the next phrase.

Beethoven considered the fifth movement (*Cavatina*) to be the masterpiece of his later compositions and the pinnacle of all of his chamber music. Karl Holtz, a violinist member of the famous Schuppanzigh Quartet, maintained a close friendship with Beethoven. According to Holtz, Beethoven "composed the Cavatina . . . amid sorrow and tears; . . . and even the memory of this movement brought tears to his eyes." Beethoven's expression mark, *Beklemmt* (afflicted, oppressed, gripping), in the latter part of the *Cavatina* has been subject to wide interpretation. The soft, steady triplet rhythm in the lower three voices is superimposed by an irregular rhythm in the first violin which is believed to express sobbings.

The recording of the *Cavatina* by the Guarneri Quartet was encapsulated in Voyager II and launched into eternity on August 20, 1977 along with other artifacts chosen to represent the best of this world's culture.

Grosse Fuge Opus 133 is the original finale of the thirteenth quartet. It was sketched in 1824 before the B flat quartet was actually conceived. The *fugue* is preceded by an introduction of 29 bars which Beethoven entitled *Overtura*. The *fugue* itself is complex. Its construction has been epitomized by Vincent D'Indy as follows: "This is a fugue with two subjects and a variation. The piece's unity is achieved by a principal theme, the counter–subject of the first fugue becoming the subject in the second."

Philosophically, Beethoven's *Grosse Fuge, Opus 133* has been projected as representing a reconciliation between two opposites: absolute freedom and necessity. This concept obviously involves in–depth analysis. As a musical composition, the *Grosse Fuge* is held in awe by most musicians. Tovey[1] esteemed it to be "incomparably the most gigantic fugue in existence."

[1]Tovey (1875–1940), Sir Donald Francis, musician, composer, editor, writer, professor of music at the University of Edinburgh.

LUDWIG VON BEETHOVEN   (1770–1827)

Opus 133   Grosse Fuge Quartet

The *Grosse Fuge*, which passes as Beethoven's sixteenth string quartet, is usually called *Grand Fugue* in Great Britain, and among chamber music players it is popularly referred to as the *Big Fugue*. Beethoven composed it originally as the sixth movement, *i.e.*, the *finale*, of the thirteenth quartet, the *Great B Flat, Opus 130*.

The *Grosse Fuge* is both difficult of comprehension and execution, yet so rugged and so noble that its effect is astonishing. In 1826, it was universally condemned; but now, in the second century after it was composed, it has found its way into sophisticated concerts, and it is probably only a matter of time for its complete appreciation and acceptance.

Beethoven's publisher, Artaria, urged him to present the *fugue* as an independent work since the movement was lengthy, abstract, and had not received popular acclaim. Beethoven acceded to his publisher's wishes and wrote a more amicable and publicly acceptable *Finale* for the *Great B Flat Major* quartet. Artaria also published the original *Finale* and labelled it as the *Grosse Fuge, Opus 133*, quartet 16.

In referring to the *Grosse Fuge*, Cobbett, in the *Encyclopedic Survey of Chamber Music*, states:

> We find in the *fugue* an opposition between two antagonistic views of Nature, one gently melancholy. . . and the other, exuberant in its gaiety.

The twenty–nine bars of introduction were entitled *Overtura* by Beethoven and precede the exposition of the *fugue*. Detailed analyses of the *fugue* have been published by a number of musicologists (Vincent d'Indy, Daniel Gregory Mason, and others). Suffice it to state that the composition is abstract and sophisticated. For many chamber music enthusiasts, including myself, the intellect is served in this amazing composition at the expense of the ear.

F. W. S. at grave of Beethoven, Vienna, Austria.

JOHANNES BRAHMS
Born: May 7, 1833, Hamburg, Germany.
Died: April 3, 1897, Vienna, Austria.

JOHANNES BRAHMS

Opus 8   Trio in B Major

Neue Ausgabe

I.   *Allegro con brio*
II.   *Scherzo, Allegro Molto*
III. *Adagio*
IV. *Allegro*

The *B Major Piano Trio, Opus 8*, was completed in January 1854 in Brahms' twenty–first year. It was the first chamber music composition that Brahms published. Americans should take special pride in this great work since it was pioneered not in Germany but in New York City.

On November 27, 1855, the Brahms *B Major Trio* was given the world's premiere performance in a Manhattan auditorium called Dodsworth Hall at Broadway and Eleventh Street. The first European performance did not take place until three weeks later in Breslau. The New York concert at which the *Trio* was played was organized by William Mason, a twenty–six year old talented American pianist who had studied with Liszt and had recently returned from an European tour. Mason had acquired a copy of the *Trio* in Europe, – hot off the press, and had brought it to America with him. His two colleagues in the performance were a twenty year old violinist named Theodore Thomas and a young cellist named Carl Bergmann. Both Thomas and Bergmann were destined to become the most distinguished orchestral conductors of their day: Thomas became conductor of the Chicago Symphony (formerly known as the Theodore Thomas Orchestra), and Bergmann became the sole conductor of the

New York Philharmonic from 1866 to 1876. Both men were responsible in large measure for the development of symphonic music in America.

It should be noted that the *Trio* played at the premiere performance in New York City is not the version that is heard today. Thirty–six years after the publication of *Opus 8*, Brahms took a second look at the work of his youth and, after much thought and self–criticism, decided that it should be revised. As a consequence, three movements of the first version were drastically revised; excepting for the *coda*, the second movement was left unchanged. With it all, it is generally agreed that Brahms managed to retain in the revision the exuberant, youthful energy of the first version and to temper it with the wisdom, grace, poise, and experience of advanced age.

The publication of the revised version(*Neue Ausgabe*) in 1891 was met with general acceptance in musical circles. The expressions of Elizabet von Herzogenberg[1] were typical of the reactions. Portions of a letter, dated October 9, 1891, that she wrote to Brahms are quoted herewith:

> I was strangely affected by the old–new *Trio*. Something within me protested against the remodeling. I felt you had no right to intrude your master–touch on this lovable, if sometimes vague, production of your youth. I decided it could not be a success, because no one is the same after a lapse of so many years. . . . I therefore made it a point of not looking at the old *Trio* beforehand. I had forgotten many parts of it and did not know where the new Brahms joined on. . . . However, I recognized your

---

[1]Elizabet von Herzogenberg was a distinguished patron of music, an excellent amateur pianist, and respected for her remarkable faculty of keen musical criticism.

insert in the first movement instantly, was completely disarmed, and played on it in a transport of delight. It is <u>beautiful</u> in its present form and I gladly leave it to the musical philologues to remonstrate with you. . . . The *Adagio* has gained wonderfully in smoothness by the contraction and the glorious, stately stride of the principal subject has lost nothing of its fascination. . . . In short, who would not welcome this piece with its wise face and youthful complexion?

Nun kann man's zweimal lesen,
Wie gut ist das gewessen!"

It is only fair to state that a few chamber music enthusiasts still prefer the earlier edition; however, most prefer the second version. The *Trio* contains a profusion of melodies with lovely, flowing subsidiary themes. Both versions remain jewels in the repertoire of chamber music. Brahms' music is generally regarded as architectural rather than pictorial. His compositions contain harmonies and melodies that bear a refined elegance and impart a type of permanent solidity that does not become boring after repeated performance. When Brahms was questioned about the origin of his musical themes, he is alleged to have replied that his best melodies came into his head while brushing his shoes before dawn.

The question is often asked, "Which of Brahms' four piano trios do you prefer?" My answer is, "The one I played or heard last."

Mason Jones, Jean Carrington Cook, and F. William Sunderman.
Brahms Horn Trio, *Opus 40*.
The Curtis Institute of Music, Philadelphia, Pennsylvania.
November 15, 1989.

JOHANNES BRAHMS (1833–1897)

Opus 40 Trio in E Flat Major

I.   *Andante*
II. *Scherzo*
III. *Adagio mesto*
IV. *Finale. Allegro con brio*

Brahms wrote sympathetically for the horn and featured it frequently in his compositions. The horn was an instrument he had learned to play in his youth and, consequently, he developed an affection for its sound. The combination of horn, violin, and piano is an unusual one since it joins a brass instrument with two chamber instruments. However, it should be noted that Brahms left an option for the "middle" voice by making an arrangement for the viola and, later, for the cello. Suffice it to note that there is almost universal agreement that the horn combination is the most appropriate one for this work.

Brahms composed the *Trio* for the natural horn, known in Germany as the Waldhorn (forest horn). The scale of the Waldhorn is obtained by playing the harmonic series as open notes and by partially closing the bell of the horn with the hand for the adjacent semi–tones. Thus, the Waldhorn player is forced to blend the open tones with the muffled closed ones, which presents many difficulties. The invention of the ventil or valve horn in the middle of the last century modernized the relatively primitive Waldhorn and removed most of the vexatious difficulties that were inherent in playing the natural instrument. Brahms, however, had intended his work to be played with the Waldhorn since he believed that its sounds had a richer quality than those produced by valves. Although the initial performances of the *Horn Trio* were undertaken with the Waldhorn, horn players have long abandoned its use and the work is performed practically always with the ventil instrument.

The initial drafts of the *Horn Trio* were made in 1862, and the work was finally completed at Lichtenthal, near Baden–Baden, in 1865. The first performance was a private one in Karlsruhe on December 7, 1865. Public performances were given in Leipzig in December 1866 and in Basle, March 26, 1867. At the Basle concert, Brahms played the piano; Ludwig Abel, the violin; and Hans Richter, later the renowned Wagnerian conductor, the horn. Years elapsed before the *Horn Trio* gained acceptance as one of Brahms' pre–eminent compositions. In a letter to Brahms dated January 5, 1879, Billroth[1] wrote,

Your *Horn Trio* has recently had enormous success. I might scarcely have expected it with this very deeply felt music, especially since the public did not listen attentively. How curious [are] those changes [in attitude] among audiences.

The first movement, *Andante*, does not adhere to the usual *sonata* form with a developmental section but is written more as a *divertimento*. The violin announces the beautiful, peaceful lyrical theme which predominates throughout the movement. Dietrich, a friend of Brahms, wrote in his *Reminiscences* that he and Brahms had been walking one day in the wooded heights above Baden–Baden and that Brahms pointed out the spot where the theme of

---

[1]Viennese surgeon and intimate friend of Brahms.

the first movement came into his mind. According to Dietrich, Brahms said, "I was walking along one morning and as I came to this spot the sun shone out and with it this theme." The movement closes with a tender benediction by the horn.

The *Scherzo* is a joyful, galloping movement requiring virtuosity for all three instrumentalists. In the trio portion, marked *Molto meno Allegro* (much slower), the horn takes over the graceful flowing melody.

The tempo marking for the third movement, *Adagio mesto*, portends its sorrowful and saddened character. The movement is based on the old German chorale, *Wer nur den lieben Gott lasst walten (He who lets only the dear Lord reign)*. Brahms' mother had recently died, and it is conjectured that the movement was intended as a requiem memorial to her. This movement is Brahms' finest. For pure beauty, there are few selections within the realm of music that can equal this immortal passage.

The *Finale, Allegro con brio*, represents a glorious change in mood. The movement depicts a joyful cross–country hunt with jolly horn calls and rhythms of the chase. To establish the spirit for this movement, the horn is indispensable and cannot be replaced. Neither the viola nor the cello arrangements can serve adequately as substitutes.

Henry Drinker has summarized our thoughts about the *Horn Trio*:

Each of the four movements is a masterpiece. . . . The most critical examination from one end to the other will disclose no weak spots. It is hard to find a serious musician who does not like the *Horn Trio*. There is but one such work.

F. William Sunderman and Josef Märkl gazing at
statue of Johannes Brahms in Detmold, Germany.

JOHANNES BRAHMS (1833–1897)

Opus 51, No. 1   Quartet in C Minor
Dedicated to Dr. Theodor Billroth

**First performance, December 11, 1873
at the Musikvereinssaal, Vienna
by the Hellmesberger Quartett**

I.   *Allegro*
II. *Romanze. Poco Adagio*
III. *Allegretto molto moderato e comodo.
     Un poco piu animato*
IV. *Allegro*

Brahms published three string quartets. Each of them, in its own way, is inimitable. The *C Minor, Opus 51, No. 1* quartet is undoubtedly the most austere and formal of the group; however, like the other two quartets, it is also a treasure that is richly rewarding for both listener and player.

The two quartets that comprise *Opus 51* were completed in 1873 in Brahms' forty–first year. Both quartets were released for publication at the same time. It is noteworthy that these two quartets are amazingly dissimilar in mood and character. The *C Minor Quartet* (*Opus 51, No. 1*) may be considered to bear a resemblance to the Beethoven Rasoumovsky quartets (*Opus 59*); on the other hand, the *A Minor Quartet* (*Opus 51, No. 2*) bears a concinnity to the elegant, romantic style of the Schumann quartets (*Opus 41*).

The *C Minor Quartet* was not the first quartet that Brahms composed; it was the first that he allowed to survive. Brahms declared that he had written more than twenty quartets before the *C Minor* and that he had destroyed all of them. Furthermore, it is said that the *C Minor Quartet* lay on Brahms' desk for a protracted period before he finally decided to release it.

The opening theme of the *C Minor Quartet* is heroic in character, – embracing in the first seven bars a series of fiery, upward surging dotted couplet rhythms (— ⌣). In

verse, the couplet rhythm of a long and short syllable is known as a *trochee*. *Trochee* rhythms pervade the entire movement into the recapitulation. The unexpected quiet ending of the first movement appears to repudiate the forceful assertiveness of the opening passages and gives the impression that the movement ran out of breath.

The pleasing second movement in A Flat Major and 2/4 tempo is structurally related to the first movement through a continuance of the *trochee* rhythm in the opening section and its recall toward the closing. This movement bespeaks of Beethoven's influence.

See example on next page.

Romanze. Poco Adagio

The body of the *Scherzo* (*Allegretto molto moderato e comodo*), written in the key of C Minor and 2/4 tempo, portrays a melancholic tenderness. The contrasting trio in F Major and 3/4 rhythm is an animated dance in the best Viennese tradition.

The fourth movement, *Allegro*, returns to the key of C Minor and begins with a forceful recall of the *trochee* couplet

Allegro

meter in the first movement. This strain eventually diminishes into calmer moods, although weighty couplets peer through the music almost to the end. Listeners will find the last movement to be an impressive closing to a quartet of chivalrous stature.

Johannes Brahms as a young man.

JOHANNES BRAHMS (1833–1897)

Opus 51, No. 2   Quartet in A Minor

Dedicated to Dr. Theodor Billroth

First performance, October 18, 1873, in Berlin by the Joachim Quartet

I.   *Allegro non troppo*
II. *Andante moderato*
III. *Quasi Menuetto, Moderato, Allegretto vivace*
IV. *Allegro non assai*

The two string quartets that comprise *Opus 51* were composed in the summer of 1873 in Tutzing, near Munich, where Brahms lived a simple, rustic life and is said to have suffered no lack of companionship from charming representatives of the opposite sex. Both quartets were dedicated to Dr. Theodor Billroth, the world famous professor of surgery in Vienna and a distinguished musician[1] and patron of music. Through the 1870s, practically all of the chamber music composed by Brahms was played for the first time before a selected audience in Billroth's home. Hanslick[2], the renowned Viennese music

---

[1]Billroth played the piano and viola. He was an excellent piano accompanist, and, during his student days at the University of Gottingen, he is said to have been the accompanist for Jenny Lind. Billroth's book, *Wer ist musikalish? (Who is Musical?)*, is a classic in its field.

[2]Hanslick's antipathy for Wagner resulted in Wagner's characterization of him as Beckmesser in *Die Meistersinger*. As a consequence, he was called the Beckmesser of Musical History at the University.

critic, humorously remarked that Billroth had *Jus primae noctis*. Throughout these years, new compositions of Brahms were given to Billroth in manuscript form for his comments. This was a flattering acknowledgment of the confidence which Brahms placed in Billroth's musical judgment. Thus, the dedication of Brahms' first two string quartets to his loyal friend and patron was overwhelmingly deserved.

Of the two *Opus 51* quartets (C Minor and A Minor), most musicians, if questioned, will state their preference for the A Minor because the melodies are more pleasing for playing and for listening. Brahms resolved many of the subtle technical difficulties of quartet writing in *Opus 51, No. 2* and brought forth a warm, lyrical, and refulgent masterpiece.

The first movement begins with a motive of four notes, A F A E, for the first violin (as shown in the illustration).

This combination is believed to have been derived from Joachim's[3] lifelong motto, *FAE, Frei aber einsam (free but lonely)*. On the other hand, Brahms is said to have preferred the motto, *FAF, Frei aber froh (single but happy)*. This opening motive assumed prominence when it became indirectly responsible for a rift between Brahms and Billroth. On one of his visits to Billroth's home, Brahms

_____

[3]Celebrated Hungarian violin virtuoso.

found the A F A E motive (in the first line) of the manuscript cut out and attached to his photograph, as a sort of autograph. Brahms became greatly displeased to find that his manuscript had been (in his opinion) mutilated. It required the diplomatic talents of Adolph Exner, the Rector of the University, to patch up the spat.[4]

The implications of the opening motive portend to the sunny, amiable character of the entire composition. The *Andante moderato* movement boasts of an unhurried, nobly eloquent theme with a suggestive Magyar feeling. The *Quasi Menuetto* movement consists of alternations of lyrical sections in 3/4 time with lively *Allegretto vivace* sections in 2/4 time. The *Finale* in 3/4 time is an hilarious *rondo* based on two beautiful opposing themes. The initial Hungarian czardas theme becomes expanded into a voluptuous waltz–like *rondo*. Daniel Gregory Mason, in his monumental treatise on *The Chamber Music of Brahms*, notes:

> In its musical content, the *A minor Quartet* displays the same easy charm as its tonal setting. Viennese *Gemutlichkeit* is more evident in it than North German earnestness.

---

[4]During a visit to the "Honored Graves" section in the main Vienna cemetery, I found Exner's grave located between those of Billroth and Brahms. This brought a smile since it appeared as though Exner was continuing his role as peacemaker. (F.W.S.)

Conservatory of Music, Detmold, Germany,
where Brahms served as a faculty member.

JOHANNES BRAHMS (1833–1897)

Opus 108   Sonata in D Minor

I. *Allegro*
II. *Adagio*
III. *Un poco presto con sentimento*
IV. *Presto agitato*

The principal outlines of the third *sonata* (the last of the violin and piano *sonatas*) were composed in 1886 at Brahms' lakeside retreat in Hoffstetten, near Thun, Switzerland. The work was completed in the summer of 1988 and was given its premiere performance in Vienna in December of that year.

Brahms spent three happy summers in succession at his Swiss retreat where he accomplished an astonishing amount of creative work. After 1889, Brahms' activities began to diminish. His appearances as a conductor became less frequent, and his concertizing as a pianist practically ceased. However, Brahms had no financial concerns, since he was a relatively rich man and his needs were minimal.

The *D Minor Sonata* is much more brilliant and fiery than Brahms' two previous violin and piano *sonatas*. The *sonata* is not only formally more advanced, but it is more symphonic in texture, more intellectually conceived, and, admittedly more difficult to perform, – technically and interpretatively. In writing the piano part, it seems probable that Brahms had in mind the virtuosic ability of the famous 19th century pianist and conductor, Hans von Bulow (1830–1894), to whom the work was dedicated. The *D Minor Sonata* is acknowledged to be one of the greatest of

163

the violin and piano *sonatas* in the world's literature. What glorious music is contained in the four movements!

The first movement begins with a beautiful melody – *sotto voce*. It is important that the initial *sotto voce* be observed since otherwise the tremendous expansion later on will not be properly perceived. The beginning theme then develops (*mezzo voce*) into a wavy exposition which, on careful scrutiny, is a repetition of the opening melody and its accompaniment. This subtle development is novel and is a display of Brahms' unusual inventiveness. The recapitulation is lengthy, ingenious, healthy, and masculine.

The *Adagio* movement is a rich, flowing, warm love–song spun in the lower register on the G string of the violin. The melody attains a series of impassioned climaxes by the culmination of magnificent double–stopped piercing chords. The movement ends in a serene, meditative, reflective mood.

The third movement is a fairy–like *intermezzo* in F Sharp Minor, – whimsical and full of tenderness. Murdoch, the musicologist, remarks that "Brahms never conceived anything more playful or more elfin than this. Happiness is everywhere." In commenting about the *D Minor Sonata*, Clara Schumann wrote in a letter to Brahms, "I loved very much . . . the third movement, which is like a beautiful girl frolicking with her lover – then suddenly, in the middle of it all, a flash of deep passion, only to make way for sweet dalliance again. . . ." Brahms probably smiled reprovingly at her analogy. To him, music was never remindful of anything excepting music.

The fourth movement is a vehement, carefully structured, and energetic masterpiece. Of all the movements in the three violin and piano *sonatas* that Brahms composed, it is generally agreed that this movement is predominant. In Murdoch's words, "It is triumphant, it is down–right, it is the work of a full–blooded man."

To this writer, the *Sonata in D Minor* typifies the character of Brahms himself. Joachim expressed it quite well, –"...it is of noble nature without vanity or arrogance."

CLAUDE–ACHILLE DEBUSSY
Born: August 22, 1862, Saint–Germaine–en–Laye, France.
Died: March 25, 1918, Paris, France.

CLAUDE–ACHILLE DEBUSSY[1]

Opus 10   Quartet in G Minor

I.   *Animé et très decidé*
II. *Assez vif et bien rythmé*
III. *Andantino doucement expressif*
IV. *Très moderé*

The magnificent revolutionary string quartet of Debussy dates from 1893 when Debussy was 31 years of age. Over the years, it has achieved a prestigious, world–wide recognition, and has enjoyed an overwhelming universal admiration among chamber music players. It is recognized that in writing the quartet, Debussy bravely ventured into harmonic territories that were unfrequented and unheard of in his time. The composition possesses creative fire and breathes an entirely new atmosphere of sound. It bears an ennobling lyricism bordering on religious veneration, while at the same time displaying an austerity of thought and a scholarly academic concern with structure.

The *G Minor Quartet* is frequently referred to as a form of impressionism, – a terminology derived from painting and literature. The term impressionism in painting implies the concept that a painting is an object in itself rather than the portrayal of an object. Music, however, is an abstract form of art and, in the writer's opinion, such terms as impressionism, symbolism, etc., are incorrectly used to explain the nature and structure of a composition such as

---

[1]Debussy's Christian name was Achille. He used his Christian name into his twenties. Later, he hyphenated the name to Claude–Achille.

Debussy's quartet. Like the string quartets of Beethoven, the fugues of Bach, or the symphonies of Brahms, Debussy's quartet belongs in the domain of absolute music in contrast to programmatic music such as Richard Strauss' *Till Eulenspiegel* or Smetana's quartet, *From My Life*.

Debussy's pioneering quartet proved to be a single venture. It would appear that he had originally intended to write more than one quartet since he had entitled the work *First Quartet in G Minor*. It is conjectured that the initial criticisms that followed the premiere performance by the Ysaye Quartet[2] on December 29, 1893 were apparently sufficient to discourage Debussy from continuing to write in the string quartet medium. The first audiences considered the work to be a series of improvisations and the critics reported it to be "vague, floating and incoherent." Later in life when Debussy was asked why he had written only one string quartet, he is alleged to have replied that in writing the work he had said all he had to say in that form.

In composing the quartet, Debussy adhered to Cesar Franck's cyclical form of composition. This is a type of tonal architecture which relies upon a generating theme to supply the expressive material for the remainder of the work. Most of the material of the quartet is derived from the opening generating theme of the first movement. This

<hr />

[2]The members of the Ysaye Quartet were Ysaye, Crickbloom, Van Hout, and Joseph Jacob. It may be noted that Debussy dedicated the quartet to Ysaye.

theme forms the melodic germ from which the quartet unfolds. An exception may perhaps occur in the *Andante* movement in which the theme becomes more obscure. The *Andante* is a sublime, moving meditation with an almost supernatural, ethereal character. On careful consideration, it becomes evident that the exceptional quality of tone color in Debussy's quartet is in large measure achieved by bowed stringed instruments which, unlike a piano, are not hampered by a tempered scale.

SIX SONATES

POUR DIVERS INSTRUMENTS

Composées par

CLAUDE DEBUSSY

Musicien Français

La Troisième pour Violon et Piano

———

A PARIS

Chez { *les Éditeurs* DURAND ET C.ie
        Maison sise au N.º 4 Place de la Madeleine
        proche des grands boulevards.

———

Cover from *Six Sonates* by Debussy.

170

CLAUDE–ACHILLE DEBUSSY   (1862–1918)

Sonata in G Minor

I   Allegro vivo
II.   Intermede (Fantasque et leger)
III.   Finale (tres anime)

The *G minor* violin and piano *sonata* is the last of Debussy's musical compositions. It forms a part of a projected set of six sonatas that he had planned to compose for different groups of instruments. Debussy lived to finish only three of the series. The first *sonata* was written for cello and piano; the second, which is actually a trio, was written for flute, viola, and harp; and the third, the *G Minor Sonata* for violin and piano. The three *sonatas* were written between the summer of 1915 and the spring of 1917. Debussy's plan was to produce works in a modern idiom that reflected the sedateness and formalism of the early French composers.

The *G Minor Sonata* was written during the period of World War I when the German army was pushing close to Paris and at a time when Debussy was fearful, depressed, and desperately ill with cancer. He spoke of himself as a "walking corpse" and lamented that he had no impulse to compose music. Despite his sufferings and depression, Debussy managed to complete the first two movements of the sonata without too much difficulty. The finale movement, however, became elusive and required repeated revisions before being completed to his satisfaction. He wrote that the main theme in the last movement kept "turning back on itself like a serpent biting its own tail." Upon completion of the work in the spring of 1917, Debussy wrote to his friend, Godet, "In keeping with the contradictory spirit of human nature, it [the sonata] is full of joyous tumult."

On May 5, 1917, Debussy and Gaston Poulet, the violinist, gave the first performance of the *Sonata* at a recital in Paris. This proved to be Debussy's farewell concert. He passed away ten months later (March 1918). The *G Minor Sonata* obviously had been written with Debussy's stoical determination to produce a masterwork despite his grave illness.

Debussy's *Sonata* does not adhere to conventional principles, but, nonetheless, it displays an aristocratic, elegant refinement. The first movement is rhapsodic, vague, and subtle, The indeterminate lines on the violin are combined with ethereal, beautiful harmonies on the piano. The movement exemplifies Debussy's credo that:

... beauty is the ultimate, the highest objective.

The second movement has been characterized as a kind of serenade without the objective of having a fair lady appear on a balcony. The movement starts with a capricious *cadenza* on the violin followed by a light–hearted theme in rhythmical *staccato* and *pizzicato* patterns. Further on, these patterns contrast with sensuous, melodic passages.

After recalling the theme of the first movement, the *finale* breaks out into a vigorous *rondo* on a theme taken from his 1909 orchestral suite, *Iberia*. It may be said that no composer was more proud of his French heritage than was Claude Debussy. He referred to himself as *"musicien francais"* and tried to portray his compositions not only as a reflection of his own personality but that of France itself.

SONATE

pour Violon et Piano

CLAUDE DEBUSSY

I

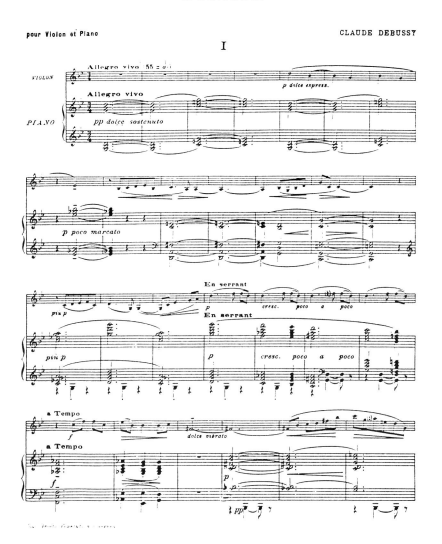

Score – Debussy, *Sonata in G Minor.*

ANTONÍN DVOŘÁK (1841–1904)

Opus 81   Quintet in A Major

I.   *Allegro, ma non tanto*

II.   *Dumka – Andante con moto; un pochettino piu mosso; vivace*

III.   *Scherzo (furiant)*

IV.   *Finale, allegro*

The term "piano quintet" obviously applies to any composition for any five musical instruments, – provided the piano is one of them. In practice, this term is usually applied to works written for string quartet with piano. There are, of course, notable exceptions, as for example Schubert's *Trout* quintet written for piano, violin, viola, cello, and double bass.

Of the 30 some chamber music compositions written by Dvořák, the *Opus 81* piano quintet in A Major[1], by popular agreement, tops the list. The composition is viewed as a faithful image of Dvořák's personality. The work possesses outbursts of beauty, joy, happiness, melancholy, and devotion, and displays Dvořák's heartfelt enchantment with Czechoslovakian folk melodies.

The first movement opens with a dreamy, pensive theme played by the cello with piano accompaniment. The theme soon expands by the addition of the other voices into a mood of buoyant happiness. The dynamic ranges extend from gentle *pianissimos* to powerful *fortissimos* with rapid changes from one mood to another.

---

[1]Dvořák also wrote another piano quintet in A Major, – *Opus 5*.

Score – Debussy, *Sonata in G Minor.*

ANTONÍN DVOŘÁK

Born: September 8, 1841, Nelabozeves, Czechoslavakia.
Died: May 1, 1904, Prague, Czechoslavakia.

174

ANTONÍN DVOŘÁK

Opus 51 Quartet in E Flat Major

I. *Allegro, ma non troppo*
II. *Andante con moto; vivace DUMKA (Elegie)*
III. *Andante con moto ROMANZA*
IV. *Allegro assai FINALE*

Dvořák achieved fame and acclaim following the publications of the *Three Slavonic Rhapsodies (Opus 45)* and the *Slavonic Dances (Opus 46)* in 1878. The popularity of these works led Jan Becker (1883–1884), leader of the famous Florentine Quartet, to request Dvořák to compose a Slavonic quartet especially for his ensemble. Dvořák complied, completed the quartet on March 28, 1879, numbered it *Opus 51*, and dedicated it to Becker.

In the early summer of 1879, Brahms introduced Dvořák to the distinguished Hungarian violin virtuoso, Josef Joachim. Dvořák showed Joachim the score of the *E Flat Quartet*, and Joachim became so impressed with the work that he not only gave the quartet its first performance in Berlin on July 28, 1879, but also encouraged Dvořák to write a violin concerto. This concerto was completed in September 1879 and dedicated to Joachim. Although the Florentine Quartet did not perform the *Opus 51* quartet publicly until November 1879, nevertheless, the Florentine Quartet was responsible for popularizing it throughout Europe and England. *Opus 51* became a favorite attraction in Victorian London where its uninhibited Slavonic melodies gave a vicarious pleasure to a society whose musical tastes and manners were as tight–laced as its women.

175

The *E Flat Quartet* gives evidence of Dvořák's enjoyment of life. Like his music, Dvořák's outlook on life was healthy, wholesome, and sophisticated. Moreover, in his pursuit of artistic excellence, he also sought to have his music appeal to all classes of society from plebeian to patrician.

The first movement of the quartet consists of Bohemian melodies and is essentially an expression of good–natured, carefree Czechoslovakian folk music. The chief theme of the first movement becomes interwoven with a joyful polka as a subtheme.

The second movement in G Minor is designated *Dumka (elegie)*. A *Dumka*[1] is literally a lament and denotes a pensive, melancholy mood. In spite of this designation, this movement contains two sections of amazingly contrasting moods. The first section is a despondent dialogue between the first violin and viola over a calm accompaniment by the second violin and harp–like *pizzicato* chords from the cello. On the other hand, the second section is a spirited, vigorous Czech dance of furiant character in G major and belies any pensiveness. In the recapitulation, both sections are presented in modified form.

The third movement bears the title *Romanze*. It is written in the key of B Flat Major and in an *andante con moto* 6/8 rhythm. The movement is a beautifully serene, wistful nocturne. Soft double–stopping in the

---

[1]The word *dumka*, pleural *dumky*, is a diminutive of the noun *duma* and is derived from the verbs *dumat, dumac* with the meaning to meditate, to ponder or brood. In the Ukraine, the word refers to poems and songs of heroic deeds.

instrumentation creates a heavenly quality of tone. The movement is indeed an exquisite expression of tenderness and warmth and must be classified as one of Dvořák's more precious musical gems.

The *Finale* has been described as "the artistic treatment of the Czech dance called the *skoena*." The movement is bright, lively, and humorous. It is written in the key of E Flat and in 2/4 *polka* rhythm. The joyousness and gaiety are particularly effective at the close.

In beauty and craftsmanship, the *E Flat Quartet* is one of the most attractive chamber music works to emanate from Dvořák's pen.

ANTONÍN DVOŘÁK (1841–1904)

Opus 81 Quintet in A Major

I.   *Allegro, ma non tanto*

II. *Dumka – Andante con moto; un pochettino piu mosso; vivace*

III. *Scherzo (furiant)*

IV. *Finale, allegro*

The term "piano quintet" obviously applies to any composition for any five musical instruments, – provided the piano is one of them. In practice, this term is usually applied to works written for string quartet with piano. There are, of course, notable exceptions, as for example Schubert's *Trout* quintet written for piano, violin, viola, cello, and double bass.

Of the 30 some chamber music compositions written by Dvořák, the *Opus 81* piano quintet in A Major[1], by popular agreement, tops the list. The composition is viewed as a faithful image of Dvořák's personality. The work possesses outbursts of beauty, joy, happiness, melancholy, and devotion, and displays Dvořák's heartfelt enchantment with Czechoslovakian folk melodies.

The first movement opens with a dreamy, pensive theme played by the cello with piano accompaniment. The theme soon expands by the addition of the other voices into a mood of buoyant happiness. The dynamic ranges extend from gentle *pianissimos* to powerful *fortissimos* with rapid changes from one mood to another.

---

[1]Dvořák also wrote another piano quintet in A Major, – *Opus 5*.

The second movement is one of the finest examples of a Dvořákian *dumka* (a Czech word for meditation or elegy). The predominating melancholic, sorrowful melody in F Sharp Minor modulates into a cheerful and tuneful section in D major. This then is set aside for a fiery dance (*vivace*) in 2/8 rhythm. The movement actually consists of a theme with four variations with interjected contrasts. It is apparent that Dvořák delighted in inserting *dumka* movements into his chamber music compositions.[2] Characteristically, *dumkas* are Slavic folk music of Ukranian origin.

The *Scherzo* opens with a lively dance in A Major and in 3/4 quick waltz tempo. The middle section in F Major, *poco tranquillo*, provides a refreshing contrast before returning to the original brilliant figure.

The *Finale* is filled with spirited melodies and lively rhythms skillfully and delicately arranged. At the close, a short *tranquillo* section precedes the brilliantly jubilant ending.

----

[2]Examples: *Dumky Trio, Opus 90*; E flat string quartet, *Opus 51*; and string sextet, *Opus 48*.

ALBERTO EVARISTO GINASTERA
Born: April 11, 1919, Buenos Aires, Argentina.
Died: June 28, 1983.

180

ALBERTO EVARISTO GINASTERA

Opus 26   Second String Quartet

I.   *Allegro rustico*
II.   *Adagio angoscioso*
III. *Presto magico*
IV.   *Tema Libero e rapsodico*
V.   *Furioso*

Ginastera was born in Buenos Aires, Argentina, and lived in that city the first 52 years of his life. During his youth, he was a music student at both the Williams and National Conservatories of Buenos Aires. At the age of 19 years, he composed a ballet and orchestral suite, *Panambi*, which was published and performed by major symphony orchestras through the world. The premiere performance of this composition was given in his native city in 1931.

At the age of 25, Ginastera was appointed Professor of Composition at the National Conservatory of Buenos Aires and was also awarded the chair of music at the Liceo Militar General San Martin. For political reasons, he was dismissed from this chair when Peron came into power in 1945.

Ginastera had been awarded a Guggenheim fellowship in 1942 but did not activate the award until 1945. From 1945 to 1947, he continued his musical studies in the United States under the terms of the fellowship.

After Peron was overthrown in 1955, Ginastera resumed his association with academe. In 1958, he was appointed dean of the faculty at the Argentine Catholic

University and, in the same year, was tendered a professorship at the University of La Plata.

During the first half of 1968, Ginastera served as a scholar in residence at Dartmouth College in New Hampshire. The following year, he became separated from his wife; married the Argentinean cellist, Aurora Natola; and during the remainder of his life settled in Geneva.

Ginastera composed three string quartets during a period of 25 years (*Quartet 1* in 1948; *Quartet 2* in 1958; *Quartet 3* in 1973). The third string quartet differs from the first two by the addition of a soprano voice part. With voice augmentation, Ginastera undoubtedly emulated the second quartet of Schonberg in which the soprano voice augments two of the four movements; Ginastera, however, inserted the voice part in four of the five movements of his third quartet.

During his early years, Ginastera became highly esteemed in Latin America and South America as a composer of music with a strong nationalistic character. With the publication of the second quartet, he deliberately set aside Latin American idioms and, as a consequence, began to achieve international recognition. According to Groves:

the critical acclaim that greeted this work (*i.e., Opus 26*) marked a turning point in his career; henceforth his international stature was universally recognized.

The second string quartet was commissioned by the Elizabeth Sprague Coolidge Foundation for the first Inter–American Music Festival held in Washington, D.C., April 18 to 20, 1958. The quartet was performed by the

Juilliard Quartet at the Coolidge Auditorium of the Library of Congress on April 19, 1958 and was reported to have been the sensation of the festival.

The composer's description of the quartet is as follows:

The first movement, marked *allegro rustico*, is in *sonata* form, having two main themes, one harsh and the other tranquil. The second movement, *adagio angoscioso*, is a song in five sections: ABCBA. It consists of a broad *crescendo* and *diminuendo*, with a climax in the dramatic middle section. The third movement, *presto magico*, is a *scherzo* with two trios. (The movement is) played with muted strings throughout, – it brings out unusual sonorities of the quartet. The fourth movement, *libero e rapsodico*, is a theme with three variations, in which each part is written as a *cadenza* for the different instruments of the quartet. The fifth and last movement marked *furioso* has a three part structure, resembling a *toccata* in its rhythmic persistence and its nervous and energetic character.

Driving, frenetic rhythms characterize the A section of the first movement. The quartet is essentially a unit with four voices at times playing the same motives and at other times with two voices playing against each other to provide a tremendously exciting, barbaric effect. Section B of the first movement, in contrast, is dreamingly canonical in feeling and provides momentary rest before returning in full force to section A.

The second movement begins slowly, *Adagio angoscioso* (sorrowfully). The motive of a minor triad followed by a raised seventh is introduced and developed into solo treatments. Gradually the mood becomes urgent, until the high point, indicated *ffff con molta passione*, is reached. Finally the passion dies, returning to the opening mood.

The third movement, *Presto magico*, is what the title implies. It is characterized by a muted, triple piano, *ponticello*, will–o–the–wisp development that leaps about like lightning. Two trios provide a little contrast, but the *magico* does not subside. The fourth movement is a theme with three variations with each instrument playing *cadenzas*. The fifth movement is closely related to the first. It is fast, furious, difficult, and virtuosic in execution.

Ginastera's quartets have been infrequently played in our country. This may be due in part to the inherent technical difficulties. It is noteworthy that no recordings are procurable at the present time.

Commissioned by the Elizabeth Sprague Coolidge Foundation
and Dedicated to Dr Harold Spivacke

2º Cuarteto de Cuerdas

ALBERTO GINASTERA
1958

I

Score – Ginastera, *Opus 26*.

EDVARD GRIEG
Born: June 15, 1843, Bergen, Norway.
Died: September 4, 1907, Bergen, Norway.

EDVARD GRIEG

Opus 27   Quartet in G Minor

I.   *Un poco Andante – Allegro molto ed agitato*
II.   *Romanza*
III.   *Intermezzo. Allegro molto marcato*
IV.   *Finale. Lento. Presto al Saltarello*

Edvard Grieg was Norwegian by birth, German by training, and Scottish by parental ancestry. After the battle of Culloden in 1746, many Scottish businessmen who were Jacobites, and loyal to the cause of the Stuarts, emigrated from Scotland. Among them was Alexander Greig of Aberdeen who emigrated to Bergen, Norway. During the course of years, the digraph "ei" in the Scottish family name became transposed to "ie" in Grieg. Alexander Greig was Edvard Grieg's great grandfather.

Edvard Grieg's mother, an accomplished pianist, gave Edvard piano lessons from his early youth. In 1858, when Edvard was fifteen years old, the Norwegian virtuoso violinist, Ole Bull, visited the Griegs and became impressed with Edvard's musical talents. Bull succeeded in persuading Edvard's parents to send their son to the Leipzig Conservatory to study piano with Wenzel, a close friend of the Schumanns, and composition with Reinecke. After four years of study at Leipzig, Edvard Grieg returned to Scandinavia to continue his musical training under Niels Gade, the Danish composer (1817–1890). It was during this period that Grieg developed an enthusiastic fervor, together with his young friend, Richard Nordraak, to further the advancement of Norwegian national music. Much of their time and efforts were spent in collecting and editing folk songs and sagas and in establishing rhythmic models from the Norwegian folk dances. Grieg soon found that he had developed a special faculty for improvising and composing in the idiom of Norwegian folk music. His point of view was expressed in a letter as follows:

> Composers like Bach and Beethoven erect churches and temples. I want, as Ibsen expresses it in one of his last dramas, to build dwellings where people might feel at home and happy. In other words, I have recorded the folkmusic of my land. In style and form, I have remained a German romanticist of the Schumann school, but at the same time I have dipped from the rich treasures of native folksongs and have sought to create a national art out of this hitherto unexploited expression of the folk soul of Norway.

After a protracted illness, Grieg decided in the summer of 1877 to compose a *String Quartet in G Minor*. This composition became his prime endeavor and occupation for more than a year. The work was composed in a charming cottage studio built by Grieg and his neighbors on the shores of the fjord at Lofthus. At the outset of his string quartet project, Grieg wrote to his friend, the Danish composer, Mathison–Hansen:

> My discontent with myself grows every passing day. Nothing I do satisfies me.... While I sense that ideas are there, I am unable to draw them out of give them shape.... But I decided that this must stop. I will accomplish something big, whatever the price.

The *G Minor String Quartet* was finally completed in September 1878 and published in 1879. Judging from his expressed determination and the prolonged labor given to the composition, it seems obvious that Grieg sought desperately to enhance his image as a serious composer of classical music while at the same time trying to incorporate within the music the natural beauty of pine forests and fjords and the joys and sorrows of the Norwegian peasants.

Grieg was a romanticist. Romanticism is more than a musical, artistic, or literary mode that passed out of fashion early in this century. It is the living experience of all who treasure the ecstatic dream behind an alluring landscape, the lurking fantasy within a mysterious design, and the haunting memory of a tender love song.

The introduction in the first movement of the quartet opens with a slow, lyrical theme that appears a number of times throughout the entire work. Cobbett credits the quartet as being unique since all of its themes are derived from the opening.

Un poco Andante

The theme itself is an adaptation of the song *Spillemaend* (*Fiddler*) taken from the first musical setting to six Ibsen poems (*Opus 26*). Following the introduction, the *Allegro* section is fast–moving, richly orchestrated, and dynamically intense. The dynamics range from *fortissimo* to *pianissimo*, sometimes occurring within spans of two bars.

The *Romanza* is a movement of exquisite beauty, sentimental in character and sprightly in texture.

The body of the *Intermezzo* is in the key of G Minor and bespeaks a vigorous, masculine Norse motif in 3/4 time. The trio is a cheerful melody in G Major in 2/4 tempo.

189

The *Finale* begins with a ponderous modification of the main theme followed by a lengthy, exciting, irrepressible, and furiously paced *saltarello*. The leaping dance rhythms are suspended toward the end by a restatement in G Major of the slow *molto* theme. The movement closes rapidly with brief, boisterous bolts.

The *G Minor Quartet* is the only complete string quartet that Grieg composed. Two movements of an incomplete *Quartet in F Minor* were found after his death. Julius Roentgen completed and edited this quartet from Grieg's notes and published it in 1908.

Cover from the *Opus 27* quartet of Grieg.

FRANZ JOSEF HAYDN
Born: March 31, 1732, Rohrau, Lower Austria.
Died: May 31, 1809, Vienna, Austria.

FRANZ JOSEF HAYDN

Opus 20, No. 2   Quartet in C Major

I.   *Moderato*
II.   *Adagio*
III. *Menuetto (Allegretto)*
IV.   *Allegro – Fuga a 4 soggetti*

Among the inimitable compositions that Haydn created in 1772, the six string quartets of *Opus 20* stand pre–eminent. The quartets are distinguished not only for their craftsmanship but also for their romanticism and beauty of form. The *Opus 20* quartets are the first ones in which Haydn actually achieved a fusion of sound in all four instruments. In doing so, he developed the basic principles of quartet composition which were utilized by subsequent composers, notably Mozart and Beethoven. It is noteworthy that in the *Opus 20* series, Haydn became more prolific in the use of dynamic markings and directions. For example, he introduced such terms as: *sotto voce*; *mezza voce*; *al rovescio* (contrasting motion); *sopra una corda* (on one string); *perdendosi* (dying away); *affectuoso*.

In the early days, the *Opus 20* quartets were popularly known by two titles, *Die Grossen Quartette* and *Die Sonnen Quartette*. The first title signified greatness while the latter originated from the frontispiece of an early edition which displayed a rising sun and was interpreted to signify Haydn's maturing talents.

The first movement of the second quartet in the series, marked *Moderato*, is an excellent example of Haydn's adoption of a polyphonic style in which the first violin does not start in the dominant role. The cello begins by playing triumphantly a glorious theme in high register in the key of C. The second violin then weaves in a *fugato* counterpart, and the viola takes over the role of the bass in the three–part opening. The first violin does not enter until the seventh bar and then repeats the main theme in the key of G. The movement is characterized by a boldness of modulations and unexpected innovations. Haydn quietly closes the sparkling first movement with a nebulous *pianissimo*.

Beginning of first movement:

The second movement, *Adagio*, is of somber beauty with an entirely different texture than the first movement. The *Adagio* opens with a four bar unison passage in C Minor of operatic stature. The first half displays an ornate, baroque grandeur filled with noble recitative phrases and *cadenzas* for the first violin. The movement then evolves into a lighter vein with a refined melodious *cantabile*. The *menuetto* follows without pause (*seque menuetto*) and emerges as a tranquil song in C Major. This is succeeded by a trio in C Minor with the melody in the cello.

The last movement is a four part canon which is a masterpiece of contrapuntal technique. The movement is labelled as *Fuga a 4 soggetti* (a fugue on 4 subjects) and is strikingly baroque in style and texture. Haydn directed that the fugue be played *semper sotto voce* until the last 36 bars when he has the movement breaking out into a glorious *forte.* Seven bars from the end, Haydn abandoned the fugal polyphony with a stirring unison passage for all four voices.

As a postscript to the quartet, Haydn added *Laus omnip. Deo* (Praise Almighty God) and then the jocular comment, *Sic fugit amicus amicum* (Thus one friend runs away from another friend). This Latin phrase refers to an 18th century witticism that a *fugue* is a musical composition in which each voice runs away from the others and the listener from all of them.

The autographed copies of the *Opus 20* quartets were at one time the prized possession of Johannes Brahms. Brahms bequeathed the manuscripts to the Society of Friends of Music in Vienna, – where they remain today.

JOSEPH HAYDN
Engraving by J. E. Mansfield.
Published by Artaria & Co., Vienna, 1781.

FRANZ JOSEF HAYDN (1732–1809)

Opus 33, No. 2   Quartet in E Flat Major

The Joke

I.   *Allegro Moderato Cantabile*
II.   *Scherzo, Allegro*
III. *Largo Sostenuto*
IV.   *Finale, Presto*

Haydn is generally acknowledged to be the "Father of the String Quartet." Although many quartets were written before Haydn's time, the earlier compositions usually featured the first violin as a soloist with the other three voices serving as the accompaniment. In Haydn's principle of *Durchfuhring*, the first violin ceased to be the dominant voice, and the quartet style became polyphonic.

Toward the end of 1781, Haydn announced that, after a lapse of ten years, he had composed a series of six quartets that were written in "a new and special way." This series was published in 1782 as the *Opus 33* quartets. The original interpretation of Haydn's phrase "new and special manner" was that it was merely a promotional selling point; however, on reflection, Haydn undoubtedly meant that he was introducing a polyphonic style of quartet writing, – a style that became accepted by Mozart, Beethoven, and other composers of the period as an approved procedure for composing classical chamber music.

The *Opus 33* quartets are known collectively as the "Russian Quartets" although there is nothing that is musically Russian about them. The name obviously was due to their dedication to Grand Duke Paul of Russia. The

Grand Duke and his Duchess lived in Vienna for a short period during which time the Duchess took piano lessons from Haydn. The royal couple was especially friendly to Haydn and, on one occasion during their residence in Vienna, they presented him with a diamond studded golden snuff box. Further proof of the Duchess' affection toward Haydn may be gleaned from a portion of a letter written 23 years after she left Vienna and had become the Empress Dowager of Russia:

> I hope with my whole heart that you will enjoy good health and that, for many years to come you will earn the admiration of all music lovers through your exceptional talent and masterpieces, an admiration you so richly deserve. . . . I beg you to regard the enclosed remembrance[1] as a token of my sincere wishes with which I am as always your ever, well–disposed (*wohl affektionierte*) Maria.

The *Opus 33, Number 2* quartet is one of serenity and classical nobility. It acquired the nickname "The Joke" owing to the humorous ending in the *Finale* movement. In the ending of the fourth movement, the main theme returns with protracted pauses between phrases in order to trick the listeners into believing that the music has ended. It is alleged that through this deceptive device, Haydn won a wager that "the ladies will always begin talking before the music is finished."

The first movement of the *Opus 33, Number 2* quartet, *Allegro moderato cantabile*, is a happy, delightful melody with a simple rhythmic motif. It is written in sonata form.

---

[1]A handsome gold ring.

Haydn introduced *Scherzos* into all of the *Opus 33* quartets to take the place of the traditional minuets. As a consequence, these quartets are often referred to as the *Scherzi* quartets. The main body of the *Scherzo Allegro* movement in the second quartet is written in a lively, rhythmic dance pattern with the trio written in a graceful Landler–like form.

The slow movement, *Largo sostenuto*, is a pleasant, warm–hearted romance and portrays a sincere depth of feeling. The finale, *Presto*, is essentially a cheerful, lively *Rondo* which continues until it merges toward the end into a solemn *Adagio* phrase of four measures. And then the prank begins. The main subject of the *Rondo* is repeated in a series of two bar phrases followed by two bar pauses. After the strain is played, Haydn inserts a three bar pause and then starts all over again with the first two measures of the melody. This sequence leaves the audience perplexed and amused, – thus, "The Joke."

Birthplace of Franz Josef Haydn.
Eisenstadt, Burgenland, Austria.

FRANZ JOSEF HAYDN (1738–1809)

Opus 54, No. 2   Quartet in C Major

I.   *Vivace*
II. *Adagio*
III. *Menuetto. Allegretto*
IV. *Finale. Adagio – Presto – Adagio*

The *C Major, Opus 54, No. 2 Quartet* is listed as number 58 in Haydn's series of quartets. The number of string quartets that Haydn wrote is still uncertain; however, most historians place it as 84. Several doubtful quartets originally credited to Haydn are now known to have been composed by contemporaries. It would, however, not be surprising if more Haydn quartets were eventually unearthed. For example, Haydn listed many of his quartet opus number is sets of three of six. It is, therefore, conjectured that he may have written more than two quartets in his *Opus 77*.

Haydn's enormous output of string quartets may be placed into two categories. The first group, comprising 37 quartets, was composed between 1750 and 1772. After a lapse of nine years, during which time no quartets were written, the second group of 46 quartets was composed between 1781 and 1799.[1] The *Opus 54* quartets fall into the second category.

The *C Major Quartet*, the second quartet of *Opus 54*, is one of twelve quartets dedicated to Johann Tost.[2] The

---

[1] The last <u>unfinished</u> quartet (*Opus 103*) was written in 1803.

[2] The Tost quartets are *Opus 54, No. 1–3*; *Opus 55, No. 1–3*; and *Opus 64, No. 1–6*.

quartet is popularly known as "Joachim's Favorite." For many years, Tost was a violinist in the Esterhazy orchestra which Haydn conducted. In 1788, Tost decided to give up his musical profession and to seek fame and fortune in Paris. As a side venture of his trip to Paris, he proposed to sell the publishing rights for Haydn's quartets (*Opus 54* and *Opus 55*) and Symphonies *Opus 88* and *89*. After a period of several months during which Haydn had received no communications from Tost regarding the disposition of his compositions. Haydn became perturbed and wrote to Jean–George Sieber, the French publisher, as follows:

Now I would ask you to tell me candidly just how, and in what fashion, Herr Tost behaved in Paris. Did he have an *Amour* there? And did he also sell you the six quartets, and for what sum?"

Tost returned to Vienna the following year as a prosperous businessman and married Prince Esterhazy's housekeeper (Maria Anna de Jerlischek). He undoubtedly compensated Haydn adequately for the compositions that he took to Paris since, after his return to Vienna, Tost requested Haydn to write six more quartets and dedicate them to "*Grosshandler* (wholesale merchant) Tost."

The *C Major Quartet* begins in an unorthodox manner with two vigorous five bar phrases, both terminated by grand pauses. After this two–trial start, the melody appears in the key of A Flat Major and then modulates through a number of key changes. The movement embraces pleasing acrobatic configurations for the first violin that reach into the clouds (high D). The movement ends with two loud C Major chords.

The second movement, *Adagio*, is a beautiful melodious song first played by violin I in an eight measure phrase and then repeated with violin II carrying the melody and with violin I assigned to a display of artistic decorations and embellishments.

Adagio

The third movement, *Menuetto*, begins with classical nobility and graciousness. The trio, in the tonic minor, is written is arpeggio form with the instruments playing in unison and progressing into amazingly modern sounding harmonies. The entire movement is in marked contrast to the *cantabile* of the second movement.

Haydn continued his break with tradition in the *C Major Quartet* by beginning the *Finale* with an *Adagio*. The charming introduction to this movement is first announced in a duet by the viola and cello and then repeated by the two violins. The melody is resumed with graceful *arabesques* by the first violin accompanied by the second violin and viola with the cello playing expressive *arpeggios* that soar into the treble register. The majestic melody of this section was later incorporated by Haydn into the *aria, mit Wurde und Hoeheit*, (With Dignity and Majesty) in his *Oratorio, The Creation*.

The *Adagio* section of the fourth movement is followed by a happy, lilting *Presto* with interesting dialogues between pairs of instruments and interrupted by two grand pauses. The *Presto* section lands on a suspended dominant seventh chord and is then followed by another *Adagio* section in reduced form. This remarkable composition ends in a mood of peace and tranquillity.

FRANZ JOSEF HAYDN (1732–1809)

Opus 74, No. 3 **Quartet in G Minor**

The Reiter

I. *Allegro*
II. *Largo assai*
III. *Menuetto. Allegretto – Trio*
IV. *Finale. Allegro con brio*

The three quartets of *Opus 71* and the three quartets of *Opus 74* should properly be known as the Salomon or the London quartets. Although all six of these quartets were dedicated to Count Apponyi, these quartets were actually written at the request of Haydn's friendly sponsor, – the highly respected London impresario, Johann Peter Salomon.

Toward the end of the 18th century, composers began to reserve the privilege of dedicating their compositions to patrons; previously, the publishers usually made the dedication. The dedication of the six quartets of *Opus 71* and *Opus 74* to Count Apponyi served as a tactful way for Haydn to thank the Count for the support and sponsorship of his application for admission into the Masonic fraternity. However, the *Opus 71* and *Opus 74* quartets bear the clear imprint of Salomon's personality and Salomon's virtuosity as a violinist. In the G minor quartet, the first violin dominates the texture of the technically difficult passages. In keeping with Salomon's personality, the slow movement is more intense and the fast movements are quicker and more restless than those of Haydn's earlier quartets.

Salomon was an 18th century German gentleman who served as the concertmaster of Prince Heinrich's Orchestra

Johann Peter Salomon, impresario.

in Prussia. Salomon moved to London in 1781 and became a distinguished impresario who arranged concerts for London audiences. He is buried in Westminster Abbey and his tablet reads, "Johann Peter Salomon /musician/ born 1745 died 1815/ he brought Haydn to England in 1791 and 1794."

The G Minor *Opus 74, No. 3* quartet has become known, over the years, as "The Reiter" quartet (horseman quartet). This appellation may be attributed to the *finale* (*allegro con brio*) movement which is filled with prancing rhythms, humorous and good natured surprises that keep listeners enraptured to the final chord. The movement starts in G Minor but turns gloriously to G Major in the recapitulation.

The mood of the G Minor *Opus 74, No. 3* quartet becomes evident from the opening *Allegro* which begins with rich octaves of powerful sonority that demonstrate its grandeur and nobility. However, it is usually acknowledged that the real soul of the quartet lies in the immortal second *Largo assai* movement. This movement, cast in ballad *Romanza* design, is justly considered as Haydn's most profound work and presages the profundity of the Beethoven *Opus 59* Rasoumovsky quartets.

Haydn was a famed favorite of London and a highly honored musician during his two visits in 1791–2 and 1794. Oxford University proudly adorned him with the white figured silk and cherry colored satin hood of the University's doctorate of music. The harmonization for *God Save Great George, Our King*, which in the United States is *My Country 'Tis of Thee*, was written by Haydn as a token of his esteem for England.

FRANZ JOSEF HAYDN   (1732–1809)

Opus 76, No. 2   Quartet in D Minor

The Quinten Quartet   Quartet # 76

I.   *Allegro*
II. *Andante o piu tosto allegretto*
III. *Menuetto. Allegro ma non troppo*
IV. *Vivace assai*

Throughout his entire life, Haydn wrestled with the problems of tonal effects that may be produced by four string instruments that are similar in *timbre* and method of sound production. Although earlier composers wrote for four–stringed instruments consisting of two violins, viola, and cello and made notable contributions in this medium, nevertheless, it is generally acknowledged that to Haydn rightfully belongs the glory of being the "Father of the Modern String Quartet." Haydn's contribution rests mainly in the adoption of a polyphonic style in which the first violin is not necessarily the dominant voice.

In 1761, Haydn was taken into the service of the Esterhazys, one of the wealthiest and most powerful Hungarian noble families of that period. The head of the family (after 1762) was Nicolaus I (referred to as the Magnificent), himself a virtuoso barytone player and a patron of music and the arts. Haydn spent thirty years at the Esterhazy Palace (Esterhaza) in Eisenstadt under circumstances that were well–nigh ideal for the development of a composer. Nicolaus II, the son of Nicolaus the Magnificent, abandoned Esterhaza after his father's death in 1790, and Haydn then moved to Vienna. After two productive periods in London (1791–1792; 1794–1795),

208

Haydn returned to Vienna and resumed his service with the Esterhazy family under Nicolaus II in 1796.

Haydn's service in Vienna under Nicolaus II was much less restrained than during the Esterhaza years in Eisenstadt. Haydn's only stipulated annual duty was to compose and direct a mass in celebration of the name–day of the Princess. Thus, the period of 1796 to 1802 proved to be an especially productive one in which Haydn composed six major masses, two oratorios (*The Creation* and *The Seasons*), and eight string quartets (*Opus 76* [six] and *Opus 77* [two]).

It would appear that *Opus 76*, consisting of six string quartets, was composed in 1796 since Haydn was alleged to have played them with friends early in 1797. However, there is some question regarding the precise chronology since the *Opus 76* quartets were not printed until 1799. The collection was first published by Andre of Offenbach and Ataria of Vienna. The latter publication bears the dedication, *"A son Excellence Monsieur le Comte Joseph Erdody de Monyorokerek, Chambellan et Couseiller intime actuel d'etat de S. M. L'Empererur et Roi."*

The second in the series of the *Opus 76* quartets is known as *"The Quinten"* or *"Fifths"* quartet. It derives its

name from the opening passage which contains two descending melodic fifths in the first violin part: A to D and E to A. The bulk of the thematic material in the first movement contains this four note idiom or at least alludes to it. The first movement adheres to the *sonata* form although it is monothematic and based on one simple idiom.

The *Menuetto* is written in D Minor with the trio in D Major. This movement is entertaining and humorous. The body of the *minuet* is a *canon* in two parts, set in octaves one bar apart. The two violins play together in octaves, and the viola and cello do likewise in imitation. Since the notes are doubled, the entire range of the string quartet is maintained.

Menuetto. Allegro ma non troppo

In Europe, the *minuet* is known as the "Witches Dance" (*Hexen–Menuett*). Cobbett pictures this movement as :

a set of brawling clowns stamping their feet tempestuously, one of them finishing after the rest. . . . – a fine example of canonical writing and a priceless piece of fooling.

The trio of the *minuet* has been aptly characterized as a chord builder. Starting with an octave in D, there is a gradual progression until a minor chord is reached and, finally the major chord of the tonic. The trio concludes with further chord building and scale flourishes by the first violin.

The fourth movement, *Vivace assai*, in 2/4 tempo, has a marvelous gypsy cast. The sparse polyphony of this movement is compensated by the exquisite figures of the accompaniment. It has been remarked that Brahms would undoubtedly have been delighted with the character of the *Finale* and especially with the triplets that appear so unexpectedly eighteen measures from the end.

The view has been frequently expressed that Haydn composed his string quartets primarily for the enjoyment of the players and only secondarily for the listening public. Be that as it may, both the performers and audience certainly owe an overpowering sense of gratitude to the "Father of the String Quartet" for providing posterity with durable, classic music of which the *Quinten* quartet is an example.

FRANZ JOSEF HAYDN (1732–1809)

Opus 76, No. 3   Quartet in C Major

Emperor Quartet
Dedicated to Count Erdody

I.   Allegro
II. Tema con variazioni. Poco adagio cantabile
III. Menuetto. Allegro
IV. Finale. Presto

The *Emperor Quartet* was composed as a convenient method of incorporating into the chamber music literature the exalted and majestic song, *Gott erhalte Franz den Kaiser*, which Haydn presented as a national anthem to his native Austria. In a visit to London in 1795, Haydn harmonized and arranged *God Save Great George, Our King* as a national anthem for the English people.[1] It was, therefore, only natural that upon his return to Vienna he should be requested by the Austrian monarchy, through the Imperial High Chancellor, Count Saurau, to compose a song "which would display before the world the true devotion of the Austrian people to their sovereign." Accordingly, Haydn chose the words of the patriotic poem by Lorenz Leopold Haschka and set them to music. On February 12, 1797, the birthday of Emperor Franz II (1768–1835), the Emperor's anthem was sung in the music halls, theaters, and churches throughout Vienna and was immediately and most enthusiastically proclaimed the official national anthem of the Austrian people. It has been said that if Haydn had

---

[1] In the United States, it is *My Country 'Tis Of Thee*.

composed nothing but this magnificent, moving hymn, his name would without doubt still have been immortalized.

The first movement of the *Emperor Quartet* begins with a tuneful melody bordering on popular folk music. Although the movement starts in sonata form, nevertheless, at about the halfway point in the movement, the theme suddenly breaks into a rustic Bohemian dance, aided by a two note drone in syncopated fifths from the viola and cello. The theme of the dance is derived from the original melody. The dance itself suggests a type of *galliardise* witnessed in servants' quarters rather than in courtly drawing rooms.

Goethe defined a quartet as a "stimulating conversation between four intelligent people." No other quartet exemplifies this definition any better than the second or slow movement of the *Emperor*. The slow movement comprises a theme and variations on the national anthem. Haydn begins the movement in a stately manner and then proceeds to place the anthem in a set of four variations, with each of the four instruments playing the melody.

For the first variation, the first violin gracefully embroiders delicate ornamentations into the beautiful melody carried soulfully by the second violin, with the viola and cello tacit onlookers. The first variation is in marked contrast with the second and third variations in which the melody is played with real dignity by the cello and then by the viola with thoughtful introspection. The final variation is a reharmonization of the anthem for all four instruments. Haydn's masterful harmonization of this last variation

Grave of Franz Josef Haydn.
Eisenstadt, Burgenland, Austria.

composed nothing but this magnificent, moving hymn, his name would without doubt still have been immortalized.

The first movement of the *Emperor Quartet* begins with a tuneful melody bordering on popular folk music. Although the movement starts in sonata form, nevertheless, at about the halfway point in the movement, the theme suddenly breaks into a rustic Bohemian dance, aided by a two note drone in syncopated fifths from the viola and cello. The theme of the dance is derived from the original melody. The dance itself suggests a type of *galliardise* witnessed in servants' quarters rather than in courtly drawing rooms.

Goethe defined a quartet as a "stimulating conversation between four intelligent people." No other quartet exemplifies this definition any better than the second or slow movement of the *Emperor*. The slow movement comprises a theme and variations on the national anthem. Haydn begins the movement in a stately manner and then proceeds to place the anthem in a set of four variations, with each of the four instruments playing the melody.

For the first variation, the first violin gracefully embroiders delicate ornamentations into the beautiful melody carried soulfully by the second violin, with the viola and cello tacit onlookers. The first variation is in marked contrast with the second and third variations in which the melody is played with real dignity by the cello and then by the viola with thoughtful introspection. The final variation is a reharmonization of the anthem for all four instruments. Haydn's masterful harmonization of this last variation yields an exceptional richness of tone and, as a hymn of praise, is capable of eliciting deep inner emotions.

The third movement is a simple, pleasant *minuet* which affords a sense of relaxation to both listener and player. The body of the *minuet* is written in the key of C Major with the trio unexpectedly switching from A Minor to A major and back again to the minor.

The *Finale*, written in *sonata* form, begins in C Minor and ends in C Major. The movement is characterized by the insertion of running triplets in all of the four parts, almost to the point of monotony. In the restatement of the theme, the key shifts to D Flat and then modulates a half tone to C Major. The *finale* is pleasing although not as effective as many of the other Haydn quartets, as for example *Opus 74, Numbers 2 and 3.*

FRANZ JOSEF HAYDN (1732–1809)

Opus 77, No. 2 Quartet in F Major

Quartet Number 82

I.   *Allegro Moderato*
II. *Menuetto Presto, ma non troppo*
III. *Andante*
IV. *Finale, vivace assai*

The two *Opus 77* quartets (G Major and F Major, respectively) were composed in 1799 and were Haydn's last completed string quartets. Both quartets were dedicated to Prince Franz Josef Lobkowitz[1], an accomplished violinist and a devoted patron of music in the Austro–Hungarian empire.

The F Major, *Opus 77, No. 2* quartet is ranked by many musicologists as one of the most notable quartets in existence. Hans Keller states:

> . . . in one or two respects, Haydn's last finished quartet tops them all, in that it simply has everything one could wish for, – all pervasive originality combined with comparatively easy accessibility, as well as great virtuosity combined with comparatively easy playability.

This superb string quartet certainly surpasses most quartets through its wealth of invention, tender lyricism,

---

[1]Beethoven also dedicated a number of his compositions to Prince Lobkowitz, among then the six *Opus 18* string quartets and the *Eroica (the Third) Symphony*. Lobkowitz's Vienna palace and residence was frequently referred to as "the Academy of Music." The residence was always open to musicians for rehearsals. Often several groups would practice in assigned rooms at the same time.

and in Haydn's display of wisdom and experience gained through a lifetime devoted to musical composition.

The first movement, *Allegro moderato*, in 4/4 meter, is characterized by its clarity of expression and its remarkable unity of structure. The opening melodies have songlike qualities. These have been attributed to the influence of writing vocal compositions (*Theresa Mass* and *The Seasons*) at the same time that Haydn was completing the *Opus 77, No. 2* quartet.

The second movement, *Menuetto presto, ma non troppo*, is actually a *Scherzo* and not a *Minuet* in the usual sense. In this quartet, Haydn reversed the order of having the slow movement second and the *Minuet* the third. The beginning of this movement, one to the bar, is delightfully boisterous and humorous. The rhythm, which has a 2/4 pulse within a 3/4 beat, creates immediate attention and interest.[2]

The principal section of the second movement is followed by an exquisitely tender and contrasting Trio in the key of D Flat Major. This *Trio* exemplifies Haydn's remarkable skill in smooth legato writing. The *Trio* and the thematically related *Coda* bear only *pianissimo* markings; however, they obviously require careful phrasing in performance. The *Coda* modulates back to the principal section in F Major.

The D Major *Andante* presents a magnificent series of variations on a beautiful melody which first appears in two part harmonization for the first violin and cello. At the

---

[2]A contemporary composer would probably have written this passage: 4/4; 2/4; 4/4; 2/4; 4/4; 2/4; etc., followed by 3/4 bars.

conclusion of the *mezza voce* violin–cello duo, the other two instruments enter softly to complete the harmonization. Halbreith states:

> The chorale–like harmonies ... [raise] ... the theme to the pinnacle of serenity and repose which will move the receptive listener to tears.

I vividly recall a glorious, unforgettable occasion of hearing this movement played in the candle–lighted Castle at Herren Chiemsee, Bavaria, as the audience walked quietly and reverently in march cadence around the heavily carpeted great hall.

The two variations that follow the main theme of the third movement are entrusted to the second violin and cello, respectively, with the first violin adding polished, graceful decorations. This movement will always remain one of Haydn's greatest masterpieces and for which an overpowering sense of gratitude is owed to the "Father of the String Quartet."

The last movement begins with a loud, sustained, sonorous chord in F Major, and thus interrupts any lingering entrancement from the previous Andante movement. The tension is released with energetic, spirited German dance themes. The movement is one of Haydn's "most boisterously intoxicating finales."

Grave of Franz Josef Haydn.
Eisenstadt, Burgenland, Austria.

FRANZ JOSEF HAYDN (1732–1809)

Trio No. 1   G Major

I.   *Andante*
II. *Poco Adagio*
III. *Finale. Rondo all'Ongarese*

The *Clavier Trio in G Major* is the first in the set of three bearing no opus number. The *Trio* was composed in 1791 during Haydn's first visit to London and is dedicated to Mrs. Rebecca Schroeter.

While in London, Haydn continued to maintain his interest in beautiful women and lost no time in forming a romantic attachment for Mrs. Schroeter, the wealthy widow of Johann Samuel Schroeter, a former music master to the Queen and one of the first piano virtuosos of Great Britain. Although Haydn was married at the time, he had long lost affection for his wife. The seriousness of his affair with Mrs. Schroeter may be gained from his own admission, "I should in all likelihood have married her if I had been single."

Undoubtedly the stimulus to compose chamber music for piano and strings during the latter part of the eighteenth century was in large measure due to the marked improvement in the tonal qualities of pianos as a result of the introduction of new technical devices in their construction. When Haydn arrived in London in 1791, he was presented with a British grand piano in which he took great pride, for it was in marked contrast to the flimsy spinets to which he had been accustomed. The English grand piano (known in France as the *piano forme clavecin*) was mechanically much more responsive, more robust, and stayed much longer in tune.

The *G Major Trio* of Haydn is the best known of his 31 trio compositions. The first movement, *Andante*, is an appealing melody which is repeated in major and minor keys with ornamentations, especially in the piano part. Tovey, in referring to Haydn's trios, states that he had the "curious inability to refrain from putting into the piano parts all that the other parts had to say"; however, he notes further that "imperfect as they are in point of integrity of parts, [the trios] are full of his grandest forms and most pregnant ideas." Similar to the first, the second movement, marked *Poco Adagio*, is melodious and displays the piano as the dominant instrument.

The third movement contains the famous *Gypsy Rondo*. This gypsy aire was probably structured from the Hungarian music that Haydn heard during his boyhood days in Rohrau. Haydn made no differentiation between Hungarian and gypsy folk music. According to Landon,[1] the gypsy melodies that Haydn incorporated into his compositions were principally those used by the Austrian Army for recruiting purposes. The Austrian officers employed gypsy bands to entice the peasant boys from the fields to the village taverns. At the taverns, the young fellows would became bedazzled by the white uniformed gypsy bands with gorgeous regalia playing stirring gypsy band music. They would also became befuddled by the Tokay wine provided for the occasions. Amid the excitement

---

[1]Landon, H.C. Robbins: *Haydn, Chronicale and Works*, volume III, Indiana University Press.

and confusion, the officers would then induce the lads to place their signature marks on recruitment forms. The young fellows frequently did not realize the significance of their commitments. Haydn was fond of gypsy aires and used them repeatedly in his compositions.

CHARLES IVES
Born: October 20, 1874, Danbury, Connecticut, U.S.A.
Died: May 19, 1954, New York, New York, U.S.A.

CHARLES IVES

String Quartet No. 1

A Revival Service

I.   *Chorale: Andante con moto*
II.   *Prelude: Allegro*
III. *Offertory: Adagio cantabile*
IV. *Postlude: Allegro marziale*

Charles Ives was born in Danbury, Connecticut. He attended the Danbury public schools and Danbury Academy and, during his boyhood, received his musical education from his father who was the town bandmaster in Danbury. His father enjoyed experimenting with musical forms by playing music in quarter tones instead of the usual half tones and by placing the musicians in the town band in the four corners of the Danbury town square to create unusual tonal effects. The unorthodox methods of Ives' father in producing music made a lasting impression on his son's later musical development.

From 1894 to 1898, Ives attended Yale University and studied composition under Professor Horatio Parker, an American born, German trained musician who achieved recognition as a conservative composer. To help pay for his education at Yale, Ives held the position as organist at the New Haven Centre Church.

Ives wrote the first movement of his first string quartet as an exercise in composition in Professor Parker's class at Yale. It is little wonder that Parker became annoyed with this young Connecticut Yankee who balked at following the accepted rules of composition. It is said that

Parker, in reviewing the first movement, exclaimed, "Why must you hog all of the keys?" Charles Ives had learned from his father to rebel against set forms in composition and to exercise independence and freedom in writing.

Ives' father died during his freshman year at Yale. Charles wrote, "Parker is a composer and widely known and Father was not a composer and little known. But from every other standpoint, Father was by far the greater man."

Ives' musical compositions were startlingly radical for his time. He engaged in polytonal, polyrhythmic dissonant writing in which individual players were urged to follow their own feelings. Many of his movements were based on hymn tunes or were fragments of folk songs and the dance tunes of his day. Most of his compositions were written between 1890 and 1922.

The first movement of Ives' *First Quartet* is based on a revival service at the Centre Church in New Haven and features two hymn tunes, From Green*lands Icy Mountains to Afric's Coral Strand* and *All Hail the Pow'r of Jesus' Name*. The composition is extremely simple and is essentially made up of notes of equal duration.

The second movement is based on a dance tune followed by a section in 3/4 time. Unexpected *pizzicatos* are injected through the movement.

The hymn, *Come, Thou Fount of Every Blessing*, is the theme for the third movement. In this movement, Ives introduces greater dissonances than in the previous two movements. *Postlude* starts with a phrase related to *Stand Up, Stand Up for Jesus*. Later he interjected the melody from the middle section of the *Prelude*. Toward the end of the movement, Ives indulged in an experiment by having the first violin and viola play in 3/4 time against the second violin and cello playing in 4/4 time.

Although the first string quartet was composed in 1896, it was not performed until 1957 and was not published until 1961.

(A Physician's Comment)

The remark is frequently made that Charles Ives is one of America's greatest composers of music. With this point of view, there are reservations.

Charles Ives spent his early life in Danbury, Connecticut. During the latter part of the last century and the early part of this century, Danbury was a center in the United States for the manufacture of felt hats. Many of Danbury's residents, working in this industry, acquired chronic mercurialism.

In the process of felting the fine hairs from the furs of rabbits, muskrats, and beavers, the smooth, straight, and resilient hairs were matted with an acid solution of mercuric nitrate using the palms of the hands to smooth down the hairs.. As a consequence, these persons became chronically poisoned by mercury through skin absorption. The disability gave rise to such descriptive expressions as "the mad hatter", "chattering away to himself like a mad hatter", and the "Danbury shakes." Bizarre emotional and psychiatric reactions were frequently observed.

Whether or not Charles Ives or his father were ever involved in Danbury's major industry has not been ascertained, so that any connection between erythismus mercurialis and Ives' off–beat compositions would obviously be conjectural. However, one might ponder upon the possibility.

F. W. S.

LEOŠ JANÁČEK
Born: June 3, 1854, Hukvaldy, North Morovia
(then Austria, now Czechoslovakia).
Died: 1928, Ostrau, Morovia, Czechoslovakia.

LEOŠ JANÁČEK

String Quartet No. 1

Kreutzer Sonata Quartet

I   *Adagio, con moto*
II.   *Con moto*
III. *Con moto; vivace; andante*
IV. *Con moto; adagio; maestoso*

Janáček (pronounced Ya–na–chek) was born in Moravia, now a part of Czeckoslavakia. He studied music in Brno (the capital of Moravia), in Prague, Leipzig, and Vienna. He married (unhappily) in 1881 and returned to Brno the following year as conductor of the Philharmonia Society and as professor of composition in the Master–school at the State Conservatoire. As a composer, he enjoyed no major success until he was 60. About that time, he fell in love with Kamila Stossl, 38 years his junior, and began an astonishingly active second youth. Throughout his life, Janáček longed desperately for recognition and believed firmly that his peculiar type of music–making would someday be vindicated. And now, more than a half century after his death, this ofttimes maligned composer has won recognition and admiration that was to a great extent denied to him during his lifetime.

Like most of the Czeck composers (Smetana, Dvořák, Novak, and Suk), Janáček's music is intensely nationalistic and is deeply rooted in Czeck folk music. However, unlike other Czeck composers, Janáček's musical contributions are completely unconventional and are filled with bold, energetic, melodic phrases that end abruptly; weird, exciting rhythms; and bizarre harmonies. Early in life,

Janáček became fascinated with the melodic phrases and rhythms of nature. He became enraptured with bird calls, animal cries, bubbling brooks, the sounds of rain and rustling leaves. It is said that he would eavesdrop on conversations in the street and jot down the musical notations of speech patterns. Conversations between his dogs were carefully transcribed onto music paper. The uniquely imaginative tonal character of Janáček's music may be attributed in large measure to the incorporation of these notations into his compositions.

Janáček wrote the *First String Quartet* between October 30 and November 7, 1923, – within the incredibly short span of nine days. He stated that the quartet was based upon Tolstoy's story, *Kreutzer Sonata*[1], which in turn was inspired by Beethoven's violin sonata, *Opus 47*.[2] The quartet was conceived as a musical poem to portray the love relationship between man and woman. In *Kreutzer Sonata*, Tolstoy ascribed immoral effects to the playing of music, as for example, "Music [is] one of the main intermediaries for

---

[1]Tolstoy's powerfully frank story of marriage and love and the discords that may ensue after marriage was related to the strange effects that may be produced by the playing of the *Kreutzer Sonata*. In Tolstoy's story, Pozdnyshev, a jealous husband, speaks about his wife's playing the *Kreutzer Sonata* with the violinist, Trukhacevski. Pozdnyshev comments, "They played Beethoven's *Kreutzer Sonata*. . . . Do you know the first *presto*?. . . . It is a terrible thing, that sonata. . . . How can that first *presto* be played in a drawing–room among ladies in low–necked dresses?

[2]Beethoven dedicated his violin sonata, *Opus 45*, to Rudolfo Kreutzer,the professor of violin at the Paris Conservatory. Kreutzer did not consider this work to be worthy of his playing and, as a consequence, he never played it in public.

encouraging adultery." On the other hand, unlike Tolstoy, Janáček sought mainly to convey, according to Josef Suk:

> . . . a moral protest against man's despotic attitude to women.

In the first movement, *Adagio con moto*, it has been assumed that the opening two bar theme is an expression of the heroine's desires and that the opening viola passage in the second movement is probably the theme of the "seducer." However, it is almost futile to try to analyze the quartet in relation to Tolstoy's story. The third movement begins as a canon between the first violin and the cello. It carries the same melody that Beethoven used at the end of the second theme in the first movement of his *sonata*. In the fourth movement, the *adagio* tune in the first movement is transformed into an emotional song, ending sadly in the key of E Flat Minor.

Unlike the chamber music of a number of his contemporaries, Janáček's music is lyrical and has listener appeal. Experienced and technically advanced amateur string quartet players will obtain enjoyment in studying this notable work.

WILHELM KEMPFF
Born: November 25, 1895, Juterbog, Brandenburg, Germany.
Died: 1991, Germany.

WILHELM KEMPFF

Opus 45, No. 1   Streichquartett

I.   *Allegro sforzato*
II.   *Menuetto*
III. *Epitaph – Adagio*
IV.   *Tempo di Bourre*

Wilhelm Kempff began his musical studies at an early age under the tutelage of his father, who was an organist and choirmaster in Potsdam. At the age of nine, Kempff entered the Berlin Conservatory and studied the pianoforte under Heinrich Barth and composition with Robert Kahn. As a result of his brilliant improvisation of a theme by Bach during his final examination, Kempff was awarded the Mendelssohn prize for piano and composition. Kempff continued his education in the arts and humanities at the University of Berlin. After graduation, Kempff's first concert tour led him to Sweden where he received the Swedish Artibus and Litteris medal from King Gustav.

Except for the years between 1924 and 1929 when he was Director of the Stuttgart Conservatory of Music, Kempff spent his life concertizing and composing music. During his active years, he made a number of world tours. His piano recitals were enthusiastically received by music–loving audiences in the major cities of the world.

Kempff's string quartet *Opus 45* was composed in Potsdam in 1942 and dedicated to his intimate friend, the classical sculptor, Arno Breker. The Märkl Quartet gave the world premier performance of the quartet (manuscript form) September 1985 at Schloss Elmau, Bavaria.

WILHELM KEMPFF   (1895–1991)

Opus 45, No. 2   Streichquartett[1]

I. *Allegro*

II. *Scherzo*

III. *Adagio*

IV. *Allegretto con variazioni on "Au clair de la lune" by Lully*

Kempff gained fame as a composer and literator and was elected a member of both the Prussian and Bavarian Academies of Fine Arts. Maestro Furtwangler conducted the premiere performance of Kempff's second symphony and the first performance of his violin concerto.

Kempff's musical compositions included two symphonies, four operas, two piano concertos, a violin concerto, two string quartets, vocal and choral works. His literary publications include *Was ich horte, was ich sah*; *Unter dem Zimbelstern*; and *Das Werden eines Musikers* (autobiography).

Kempff composed his E Flat Major quartet in 1942 upon his return from Paris where he had met several artists, including Rodin, the painter, and Cortot, the pianist, to whom this work is dedicated. This Franco–German gathering ended with a merry evening where somebody started to sing Lully's air, *Au clair de la lune*. Kempff sat down at the piano and played a series of impromptu variations to the melody. After returning to

---

1This quartet is being published by the Tongerverlag in Cologne and should soon be available for purchase. It is only recently that I have had access to this work.   F.W.S.

Potsdam, he incorporated these variations into his second string quartet.

The first movement alternates between serious *expressivo* and lyrical moods. The slow movement is relatively short but is deeply moving. The second movement is written in the form of a *Bolero* in which the two violins play the melody in canon form to a *Bolero* rhythm.

ZOLTAN KODÁLY
Born: December 16, 1882, Kecskemet, Hungary.
Died: March 6, 1967, Budapest, Hungary.

234

ZOLTAN KODÁLY

Opus 10 Quartet

I.   *Allegro*
II. *Andante – Quasi recitative*
     Allegretto; Allegro giocoso

Kodály, the composer, based his classical works essentially on Hungarian folk songs. He and his fellow countryman, Bartók, were in large measure responsible for establishing in Hungary a nationally–based high level of musical culture.

Kodály's boyhood was spent in the musical environment of Szob, Galanta, which is now a part of Czechoslovakia, where his father worked for the Hungarian state railway and played the violin. His mother was an accomplished pianist and singer. As a child, Zoltan learned to play the violin, viola, and cello proficiently and took an active part in performances of school and church concerts. He also sang in the church choir and began to compose music. His first composition, *Overture in D Minor for Orchestra*, was performed in Szob in February 1898.

In 1900, Kodály entered Budapest University as a student in the liberal arts. At the same time, he also studied musical composition at the Budapest Academy of Music with Hans Koessler. Koessler was a stimulating German teacher and scholar whose students included Bartok and Dohnanyi. Kodály received a Ph.D. degree in 1906 from the University for his thesis on the stanzaic structure of Hungarian folk music. After postgraduate studies in Berlin and Paris, he returned to Budapest in 1908 as a professor of composition at the Academy of Music. He spent most of his life at the Academy as a teacher and composer, with unavoidable interruptions owing to the wars, revolutions, and political upheavals.

Kodály maintained a lofty stature as a composer and scholar throughout his entire life. He made frequent trips abroad as a conductor of his orchestral works and appeared in the United States in 1947. Between 1950 and 1967, he published a five volume treatise, *Corpus Musicae Papilaris Hungaricae*, which served as a basis for musical education in the elementary schools of Hungary. His educational ideas became crystallized in the so–called "Kodály Method" which evolved from his 32 years of research in folk music. The basic principle of Kodály's method utilizes corporate singing for the advancement of musical literacy. Without doubt, Kodály should be ranked as one of the most important musical educators of the twentieth century.

The man who probably knew Kodály's music best was Bartók. Bartók wrote as follows:

Kodály's compositions are characterized in the main by rich melodic invention, a perfect sense of form, a certain predilection for melancholy and uncertainty. He does not seek Dionysian intoxication – he strives for inner contemplation. . . . His music is not of the kind described nowadays as modern. It has nothing to do with the new atonal, bitonal and polytonal music – everything is based on the principle of tonal balance. His idiom is nevertheless new; he says things that have never been uttered before and demonstrates thereby that the tonal principle has not lost its *raison d'etre* as yet.

Kodály's second quartet has only two movements. The first movement, *Allegro*, opens with a brief introduction followed by a theme played in sixths by the first violin and cello against an *ostinato*, a persistent musical figure, played by the viola. This leads to a third section and to a stirring recapitulation of the first subject.

The second movement opens with a series of ninth chords and a *cadenza*. After the initial theme by the first violin followed by the cello, the second violin interrupts with a jolly dance melody, which is the principal theme of the *rondo*.

It is generally agreed that the reason the Kodály second quartet is infrequently heard is due to the technical difficulties that must be overcome to play it well.

FELIX MENDELSSOHN–BARTHOLDY
Born: February 3, 1809, Hamburg, Germany.
Died: November 4, 1847, Leipzig, Germany.

FELIX MENDELSSOHN–BARTHOLDY

Opus 12   Quartet in E Flat Major

I.   *Adagio non troppo. Allegro non tardante*
II. *Canzonetta. Allegretto*
III. *Andante expressivo*
IV. *Molto allegro e vivace*

Elegance, nobility, refinement, precocity, brilliancy, imagination, and felicity are a few of the hallmark characteristics of Felix Mendelssohn–Bartholdy, – the composer, pianist, organist, conductor, and musical idol of Germany and England during his adult years. It has been said that he was born under a lucky star with a silver spoon in his mouth. Materially, the Mendelssohn family was rich. They were not as wealthy as the Rothchilds, the other rich German–Jewish family, but were a close second. Felix Mendelssohn was the grandson of the Jewish philosopher and silk merchant, Moses Mendelssohn; he was also the son of a cultured Berlin and Hamburg banker, Abraham Mendelssohn. His mother, whose maiden name was Leah Salomon, was intellectual, spoke four languages fluently, and was an accomplished pianist and teacher. After her marriage to Abraham, Leah professed the Lutheran creed and raised her four children in the Christian faith. Her husband accepted Protestantism, was baptized, and added Bartholdy to his name in order to distinguish his Christian family from the other branches of the Mendelssohn kin. The name Bartholdy had been associated with Leah's family estate. It may be noted that Felix Mendelssohn retained his adherence to Lutheranism throughout his entire life.

The *Quartet in E Flat Major* was composed during Mendelssohn's twenty–first year and bears the completion date "London, Sept. 14:1829." The quartet was originally dedicated to B.P. (Betty Pister, a friend); however, after Betty's marriage to Rudorf, Mendelssohn requested Hofmeister, the publisher, to alter the dedication to B.R. by merely adding a *Federschwanz* (feather–tail) to the P. The quartet is a product of the jolly, carefree period in Mendelssohn's life when he travelled for the first time in England, Scotland, and Wales.[1] This journey provided the inspiration for the *E Flat Quartet*; an organ composition for his sister Fanny's wedding; and two major orchestral works, – the *Fingal's Cave Overture* and the *Scottish Symphony*. Although the *E Flat Quartet* is listed as *Opus 12*, nevertheless, it was actually written two years after the *Quartet in A Minor* which is listed as *Opus 13*.

Adagio non troppo.   Allegro non tardante.

The *Adagio* introduction to this movement bears a striking resemblance to the introduction of the first movement of Beethoven's tenth quartet, *Opus 74* (*The Harp*). Both introductions are weighty; both are written in the same key with similar motifs followed by main melodious themes in *Allegro tempi*. Although there is a structural similarity of the first movement of the two quartets, nevertheless, it should be noted that the works subsequently develop into widely different patterns and are wholly dissimilar.

---

[1]Mendelssohn visited Great Britain ten times during his short lifetime and regarded England as his second home.

The unusual notation, *non tardante*, in the first movement simply means "not to be held back." This is probably precautionary owing to the four *ritardante* inserted at different places into this section of the movement. The entire movement is an expression of eloquence in which the first theme maintains the dominant role. A subordinate theme in F Minor of simple purity appears in the movement, reappears in the *coda*, and is repeated again in the *Finale*.

Canzonetta: Allegretto.

For the second movement, Mendelssohn substituted the usual *scherzo* of classical quartets with a light hearted, animated, dancing *Canzonetta*, bearing a folksong type of melody. The trio in the *Canzonetta* recalls the dance of the elves in Mendelssohn's *Midsummer Night's Dream*. It consists mainly of a playful dialogue between the two violins over sustained notes of the viola and cello. The two lower instruments eventually join the frolic with a transition to the folk melody. This movement is refreshingly charming and has immense audience appeal.

Andante expressivo.

The third movement of the quartet in the key of B Flat Major leads to a more somber mood. In essence, it is a beautiful, simple song of thanksgiving. The repeated phrases of the melody in ascending triads are closely related to the introductory *Adagio* of the first movement. The hesitant ending may be explained by the *Attaca* (to bind together) notation by which this movement is joined without pause into the *Finale*.

The *Finale* (*molto allegro e vivace*) is not written in the anticipated key of E Flat but in its relative C Minor. The beginning in 12/8 meter is announced by two broad chords succeeded by a fugal form of composition from which emerges the principal theme of the fourth movement. This theme proceeds as a breathless *saltarello* to the *coda* when there is an abrupt change to 4/4 meter and to the E Flat key. The coda of the *Finale* is one of the loveliest, most radiant and lingering passages to be found in quartet literature. This passage "penetrates the ear with facility and quits the memory with difficulty."

Felix Mendelssohn–Bartholdy and his sister, Fanny.
From a painting by R. Poetzeiberger.

FELIX MENDELSSOHN-BARTHOLDY

(1809–1847)

Opus 44, No. 1   Quartet in D Major

The Christmas Quartet

I.   *Molto Allegro vivace*
II. *Menuetto: Un poco allegretto*
III. *Andante expressivo ma con moto*
IV. *Presto con brio*

The *Opus 44* quartets are three in number and were composed during 1837 and 1838. *Opus 44, No. 1* in D Major was the last to be completed and is dated July 24, 1838. The chronological order of composition is 2, 3, and 1. The three quartets were dedicated to the Crown Prince of Sweden.

It is conjectured that the *D Major Quartet* was Mendelssohn's favorite in the series, which would help to explain the order in which the quartets were designated. In a letter to Ferdinand David, an eminent violinist at that time, Mendelssohn wrote,

I have just finished my third quartet, in D major, and like it very much. I hope it will please you as well. I think that it will, since it is more spirited and seems to me likely to be more grateful to the players than the others.

Among chamber music players, the quartet is frequently referred to as *The Christmas Quartet.* Christmas was a joyous occasion in the Mendelssohn household; spirited chamber music was played (particularly the *D Major Quartet*) and gifts were lavishly given.[1]

---

[1]The *Opus 44, No. 1* quartet has been played in my home every Christmas for more than 50 years.   F. W. S.

The first movement is spirited, exuberant, and invigorating. The opening theme is happy, gay, and extroverted and is followed in contrast by a more restrained secondary theme. However, after the development, the high tension and animation are maintained with few releases, until the end.

The second movement is a charming, gentle, and melodious *Menuetto* which exerts a calming influence after the high–powered first movement. The middle section contains a series of running passages, principally allotted to the first violin, and is followed by a return to the first part.

The *Andante* movement is written in sonata form and contains charming counter–melodies for both the first and second violins. The mournful character of the third movement is quickly dispelled by the tumultuous *Finale*, *Presto con brio*. This movement is filled with rapid triple dotted rhythms resembling the *saltarello*, a vigorous 16th century Italian dance. The music in this movement is vivacious, exuberant, and exhilarating in keeping with the Christmas spirit.

Early Mendelssohn Quartet (discovered in 1944).

This quartet was discovered by Dr. Arnold Kvam, a friend and head of the Music Department of Douglas College, Rutgers University, New Brunswick, New Jersey. Colonel Kvam found the manuscript in a salt mine after World War II while serving as the music and art adviser in the Army of Occupation. The original manuscript is in the British Museum.

First page of Violin I.

245

WOLFGANG AMADEUS MOZART
Born: January 27, 1756, Salzburg, Austria.
Died: December 5, 1791, Vienna, Austria.

WOLFGANG AMADEUS MOZART[1]

K. 387   Quartet in G Major

I.   *Allegro vivace assai*
II.   *Menuetto Allegro*
III.   *Andante cantabile*
IV.   *Molto Allegro*

Mozart composed the first six of the ten celebrated quartets between the years of 1782 and 1785. These six quartets, of which the *G Major* is the first in the series, were given a flowery dedication in Latin to "My dear friend, Haydn."

The so–called "Haydn Quartets" by Mozart were patterned after Haydn's six Russian quartets, *Opus 33*.[2] The six Mozart quartets are not only proof of Mozart's inventive genius, but they also represent a lasting tribute to Haydn. Mozart learned from Haydn the difficult art of quartet writing in which the parts for the four stringed instruments are each of equal importance and are played as a unit.

---

[1]Mozart's baptismal names were Johan Chrysostomus Wolfgang Gottlieb. In his youth, he was known as Wolfgang Gottlieb. Later he changed his name to Wolfgang Amadeus since he felt that the latter combination was more euphonious and poetic. The name, Amadeus, is the Latin for Gottlieb.

[2]The *Opus 33* Haydn Quartets are entitled the "Russian Quartets" because it is alleged that they were played for the first time in the apartments of the Grand Duke and Duchess of Russia on the occasion of their visit to Vienna. The Grand Duke was the son of Catherine the Great. He became Emperor Paul I of Russia in 1796 and was assassinated in 1801.

The *G Major Quartet*, completed on December 31, 1782, is written in *sonata* form. The exposition in the first movement begins with 24 measures of a bright, happy melody followed by a subsidiary section announced by the second violin, and then by a sprightly closing section. The developmental and recapitulation portions in the first movement are characterized by clarity and elegance in style.

In the *Menuetto* second movement, Mozart proved himself to be a non–conformist, since the *minuet* mood of the ballroom was gracefully swept aside. In the chromatic opening passage, Mozart accented off–beats and made the *minuet* virtually undanceable. The effect of alternating *piano* and *forte* quarter notes, as illustrated, provides a

Allegro   *Violin I*

rhythm which is essentially 2/4 instead of the usual 3/4 rhythm of the classical minuet. The trio, written in the tonic minor, combines unison passages with rich harmonies.

The emotional high point of the quartet, in our opinion, is the slow movement. This movement is in essence a beautiful *aria* for the first violin embroidered with conversational accents of the other three voices.

The *Finale* is written in *fugal sonata* form. The theme is played first by the second violin and it then taken up in sequence by the first violin, the cello, and the viola. The *Finale* is reminiscent of the last movement of *The Jupiter, Symphony No. 41.*

WOLFGANG AMADEUS MOZART (1756–1791)

K. 428   Quartet in E Flat Major

I.   *Allegro ma non troppo*
II. *Andante con moto*
III. *Menuetto. Allegretto*
IV. *Allegro vivace*

Mozart's string quartets may be readily divided into two groups: (1) the early quartets of which there are sixteen, including two *divertimenti*; and (2) the later celebrated (*beruhmten*) quartets of which there are ten.

Mozart's first quartet, *K. 80,* was written in 1770 at the age of fourteen. The remaining fifteen early quartets were written between 1770 and 1774. Nine years elapsed before Mozart resumed his writings of string quartets. He became inspired to compose again in the medium through the influence of Haydn. Haydn's Russian quartets, *Opus 33,* appeared in 1781 in which Haydn presented a newer approach to quartet writing by advocating the principle that equal value should be given to each of the four instruments, Using this principle, Mozart began his second series of ten quartets in 1782. The first six quartets were dedicated to "My dear friend, Haydn"; the eighth, ninth, and tenth were dedicated to Friedrich Wilhelm II, King of Prussia (and a cellist); and the lone seventh quartet was dedicated to Mozart's publisher, Hoffmeister. Mozart's six quartets dedicated to Haydn were written between 1782 and 1786, In the Haydn dedication, Mozart remarked that the quartets were the "fruits of long and arduous work."

The *E Flat Major Quartet, K. 428,* is the third quartet of those dedicated to Haydn. The quartet is colloquially known as "The Octave" because of the two note octave couplet for all four instruments in the opening bar followed by a passage in the next three bars in which the two violins and the viola and cello play in unison one octave apart.

Allegro ma non troppo.

The first movement begins in a pensive mood which becomes quickly dispelled into a brighter, happier, and animated theme.

The slow movement in A Flat Major and 6/8 rhythm bears a romantic cast. It is frequently remarked that the harmonic effects in this movement seem to foretell certain passages of Wagner's *Tristan*. The movement is unique in its extensive use of chromatic progressions.

The main body of the *Menuetto* movement is cheerful and spirited. On the other hand, the trio has a somber character which is reinforced by a droning bagpipe type of accompaniment.

The *Finale* is filled with joyful good humor. The melody is catchy, and many years ago formed the basis of the popular song, *Ja–Da*.

The *E Flat Major Quartet* was written eight years before Mozart's early death at the age of 35. The available historical accounts of Mozart's fatal illness have been evaluated by my son, F. William Sunderman Jr., M.D. He ventures the opinion that Mozart must have suffered from acute glomerulonephritis, despite the recurrent speculations that he might have been poisoned with mercuric chloride by his archrival, Antonio Salieri.[1] Dr. Sunderman Jr. further states:

Following a febrile illness during the autumn of 1791, Mozart gradually developed profound weakness, pallor, edema, and relapsing uremic coma. Despite the ministrations of the renowned Doctors Closset and Sallaba, Mozart died on December 6, 1791. Mozart's last utterances were the drum passage from his famous *Requiem Mass*, which lay unfinished on his quilt. Mozart implored his wife, Constanza, to keep his death secret until his friend, Albrechtsberger, could apply to succeed him as choirmaster at St. Stephen's Cathedral. After a simple funeral at the Cathedral, Mozart's corpse was given a third–class interment. It was a wintry evening with heavy snow and, although several mourners accompanied the hearse to the city gate, no one went as far as the cemetery. Mozart's coffin was placed in a common grave, and its location was not recorded.

---

[1]Salieri was Court Kappellmeister in Vienna, 1788–1824.

WOLFGANG AMADEUS MOZART (1756–1791)

K. 454   Sonata in B Flat Major, No. 15

I.   *Largo – Allegro*
II. *Andante*
III. *Allegretto*

The *B Flat Major sonata* was hastily composed by Mozart in April 1784. It was written for a ravishingly attractive and talented 20 years old Italian violinist from Mantua named Regina Strinasacchi, who was scheduled to give a recital at the National Court Theatre in Vienna on April 29, 1784. Mozart wrote to his father,

> We now have the famous Mantuan lady Strinasacchi here, a very good violinist.... I am working on a sonata which we shall be playing in the theater on Thursday.

Mozart had met this charming feminine violin virtuoso and had apparently become enamored with her playing ability since he himself appeared at the recital as her piano partner. For some unknown reason, Mozart was obliged to play the piano part without a copy of the notes and with only some memoranda jotted on a sheet of paper in front of him. The performance came off exceptionally smoothly and securely and was acclaimed to have been a phenomenal success. Emperor Joseph attended the concert and, having observed that Mozart played without the benefit of a manuscript, requested a copy of the piano score. It is said that Mozart could only provide him with blank music sheets.

The *B Flat sonata* is a romantic, gracious composition with a violin part that is almost as demanding as a concerto. Both parts require technical precision and a careful rendering of contrasting moods and shadings of expression. The sonata itself is a delightful interplay between the violin and piano voices. The piano and violin lead and follow each other in sequences and in compatible, happy dialogues. There is abundant opportunity in performance for both instrumentalists to display independent virtuosity.

The first movement is majestic. It begins with a pompous, noble *Largo* consisting of only 12 bars before starting the brilliant *Allegro* section. Alfred Einstein, the musicologist, comments that the *Allegro* portion is approached from "a proud *Largo* through a triumphal arch." The thematic material is light, gay, and intimately conversational.

The *Andante* movement is a graceful, sympathetic violin and piano duo. The movement is deeply emotional combined with charming brilliance.

The *finale Allegretto* movement, in contrast, is a joyous *rondo*. The *rondo* theme is repeated four times with a variety of intervening surprises.

During his brief career, Mozart spun out approximately 40 violin sonatas in addition to well nigh 50 symphonies, 20 operas, 27 string quartets and quintets, and a large quantity of other music. Kochel's catalogue records roughly 600 authentic compositions. For Mozart, composing music was as effortless as it was painful to Beethoven.

WOLFGANG AMADEUS MOZART (1756–1791)

K. 458   Quartet in B Flat Major

The Hunt

I. *Allegro vivace assai*
II. *Menuetto moderato*
III. *Adagio*
IV. *Allegro assai*

The *B Flat Quartet* is the fourth in the series of six quartets which Mozart dedicated to Haydn. When one of Mozart's friends expressed surprise at the dedication, Mozart is said to have replied that he owed the dedication to Haydn since Haydn had taught him how quartets should be written. In Germany and Austria, the *B Flat Quartet* is known as the *Jagd Quartett*; in our country and England, it is *The Hunt*.

Giving nicknames or artificial titles to compositions is ofttimes a useful means for easy reference. Sometimes the titles are not clearly descriptive and, indeed, they may be misleading. However, in the case of the *B Flat Quartet*, the appellation, *Hunt* quartet, is fittingly descriptive.

The rollicking, spirited hunting call in 6/8 rhythm in the beginning of the first movement immediately suggests a jovial, merry chase. The initial hunting call is played by the two violins to simulate a pair of trumpets. It should be noted that horns and trumpets of the eighteenth century had no valves, which accounts for the fanfare type of melodies to which they were limited. It is inferred that the hunting theme for the quartet came to Mozart's mind as a result of his preoccupation at the time in composing horn concertos for the Viennese horn player, Joseph Leutgeb.[1]

The material that Mozart used in composing the first movement is, in fact, meager; however, the skill with which the material is presented causes this meagerness to be passed over almost unnoticed. Cobbett called attention to the absence of a subsidiary theme and to the "capricious play that is made up of snippets of themes." The entire movement has an open–country, fresh air atmosphere. At the 26th bar, the theme played by the second violin and viola certainly gives the impression of a pair of horns sounding off over a trill by the first violin. The passage that brings the first movement to a close is another horn call heard over a long–held drone note by the cello and resembling the bagpipe–like drones which Haydn was fond of inserting in some of his quartets.

The *Menuetto* is a deliberately rigid, gallant, courteous rhythmic dance in the early conventional style. The trio moves with a graceful dignity and poise. The entire movement is reminiscent of the early minuets introduced into the court of Louis XIV of France by Lully in the middle of the seventeenth century.

---

[1]Leutgeb was regarded as an excellent horn player but also somewhat of a yokel. Mozart took occasion to make him the butt of some of his musical jokes. For example, the tempo of the first movement of the *Horn Concerto, No. 1 (K. 412)* is designated *Allegro*, but the horn part is prankishly marked *Adagio* to call attention to Leutgeb's tendency to drag the tempo. Leutgeb, a fellow Salzburgian, supplied Mozart with faithful, loyal comraderie; Mozart supplied Leutgeb with horn concertos and immortality.

The slow movement is a jewel in romantic musical expression and an outstanding feature of the entire work. It is one of Mozart's richest and most emotionally intense compositions. The melody is aristocratic, dignified, and encompasses a spirit of heavenly peace. The opening theme becomes at once recognizable, since it was incorporated a number of years ago into the popular song, *Moonlight and Roses*.

The *Finale* is in modified *sonata* form. It is noteworthy that the beginning of the exposition and closing of the recapitulation are essentially *rondos*. The theme of the movement is said to have been taken from an old folk song. The *Finale* returns to the joyous gaiety of the first movement. In Cobbett's words, the movement is a "happy combination of delicious Mozartian roguishness and Haydnesque humour."

WOLFGANG AMADEUS MOZART   (1756–1791)

K. 465   Quartet in C Major

I.   *Adagio – Allegro*
II.   *Andante cantabile*
III. *Menuetto*
IV.   *Allegro molto*

Mozart's father, Leopold, visited his son in Vienna in February, 1785. In order to entertain his father during the visit. Mozart arranged an evening of chamber music on February 16 in which two of his recently composed string quartets, *G Major, K. 387* and *C Major, K. 465*, were played from the manuscripts. The players included himself and three renowned composers living in Vienna at the time. They were Franz Josef Haydn, first violin; Karl Ditters von Dittersdorf, second violin; Mozart, viola; and Jan Baptist Vanhal, cello.

Leopold Mozart was exceedingly delighted with the performance and wrote a description of the musical affair to his daughter, Nannerl, who was living in Salzburg. The elder Mozart reported that Haydn had spoken to him during the evening and had paid Wolfgang a most generous tribute:

> I tell you calling upon God as a witness, and speaking as an honest man, your son is the greatest composer known to me either in person or by name. He has taste, and what is more, the most profound knowledge of composition.

A deep friendship and mutual respect had evolved over the years between Mozart and Haydn. Mozart dedicated his first six *beruhmten* (celebrated) quartets to Haydn with the acknowledgment that "It was from Haydn that I first learned how to compose a quartet."

257

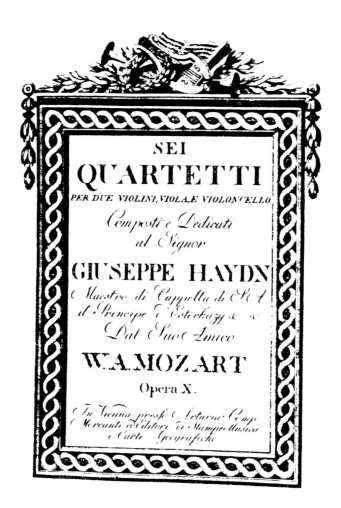

Title page of the six string quartets dedicated to Haydn.

The *C Major Quartet* is almost always referred to as "*The Dissonant*" because of the 22 bars of the slow melancholic introduction in the first movement. This section involves remarkable resolutions between dissonance and consonance. The false harmonic relations in the introduction became the center of prolonged critical debate over the years, since the dissonances were disturbing to conventional ears and confounded both critics and listeners. The unusual introduction finally evolves into a radiant, happy *Allegro* mood in C Major, which Alan Rich, the music critic, likens "to the sun bursting through the clouds."

The beautiful *Andante* movement embraces three tender themes.

The middle theme serves in the transitions.

The transitions are graceful and logical. Romance pervades the entire movement. Similar to the ending of the first movement, the *Andante* movement also ends in a *pianissimo* (*pp*).

The *Menuetto* movement portrays a somewhat somber mood with occasional brusque accents. The trio in C Minor displays an operatic conversational character with impulsive romantic questions and answerings.

The *Finale* is graceful, gleeful, and, in parts, playful. Throughout the awesome Mozartian vigor and ingenuity become evident. The *C Major Quartet* is among the top–ranking string quartets in the chamber music literature.

WOLFGANG AMADEUS MOZART (1756–1791)

K. 515 Quintet in C Major

I.   Allegro
II. Menuetto – allegretto
III. Andante
IV. Allegro

Mozart's principal occupation in the early part of 1787 was the creation of the opera *Don Giovanni*. However, in the midst of this major endeavor, he found time to compose two superlative chamber music compositions, the *C Major* and the *G Minor String Quintets* (*K. 515* and *516*). Mozart entered the *C Major Quintet* in his catalogue on April 19, 1787 and the *G Minor Quintet* on May 16. Both quintets embody the most mature and deepest expressions of Mozart's unparalleled musical talents.

It has been held that the *C Major* and *G Minor Quintets*, composed less than a month apart, were conceived by Mozart as a release of two contrasting emotional reactions: the *C Major Quintet* symbolizing optimism, confidence, and well–being; the *G Minor Quintet* symbolizing pessimism, introspection, and an obsession with death.[1] Be that as it may, both quintets are acknowledged to be peerless masterpieces.

---

[1]In a letter to his father, Mozart wrote on April 4, 1787, "... I have now made a habit of being prepared in all the affairs of life for the worst. As death, when we come to consider it closely, is the true goal of our existence, I have formed, during the last few years, such close relations with this best and truest friend to mankind, that his image is not only no longer terrifying to me, but is indeed very soothing and consoling."

The Märkl Quartet with F. William Sunderman as guest artist.
Josef Märkl, F. William Sunderman, David Johnson,
Bernhard Pietrella, and Manfred Becker playing
the Mozart *C Major Quintet, K. 515.*
Gettysburg College, Gettysburg, Pennsylvania
First concert under the Sunderman Chamber Music Foundation.
May 19, 1984.

Speculations have been made as to reasons that Mozart introduced viola quintets, an unfamiliar medium, into the field of chamber music. It has been conjectured that he sought a musical form that would yield a stronger and greater depth of sound than the string quartet and yet would remain just as distinctive. Moreover, within a framework of five instruments, a quintet would be sufficiently small to permit individual flexibility and virtuosity in performance. In addition, the tonal and contrapuntal enrichment provided by the second viola fulfilled his desire for musical expression at that period in his life. For whatever the reasons, Mozart, Brahms, and Schubert all surpassed their best quartet writing with their string quintet compositions. It might be mentioned that Joseph Haydn, when asked why he had not written for five string instruments, answered, "Because I was never commissioned to write a quintet."

The *C Major Quintet* is the longest of Mozart's chamber music compositions that embrace four movements. The first and last movements are the longest; both are marked *Allegro*, both contain a wealth of melodies and impart cheerful exuberance. The *Allegro* of the first movement contains a *stretto* type of momentum, *i.e.*, a feeling of acceleration. When the quintet was originally published, the first movement was criticized because Mozart had deviated from the prevalent principles of writing musical phrases in multiples of four bars. Mozart metered the beginning of the *Allegro* in phrases of five bars.

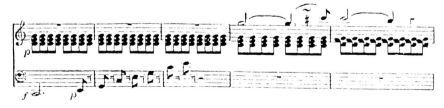

Since the initial phrase ends on the nineteenth, Mozart inserted a one bar rest for the twentieth measure in order to maintain five bar sequences.

In most of the chamber music compositions of the eighteenth century, the *minuet* movement is placed second, and the *C Major Quintet* is no exception. The *minuet* in the *C Major Quintet* is in classical form. It imparts a conversational style that anticipates the duet that follows in the *Andante* movement. The trio, written in the subdominant key (F), has a tranquil song–like character.

The *Andante* movement is exceedingly personal and is believed to portray Mozart, the viola player, as he would like to be remembered. The movement is cast in the form of a sensuous duet with floating *arabesques* of sound between the first violin and the first viola. In essence, it represents a warm, inspiring, and sympathetic dialogue between two noble instruments, discreetly accompanied by the other three voices. The *Andante* stands as a paragon in chamber music composition.

The concluding *Allegro* recapitulates the energetic pattern of the first movement. The movement is a mixture of *rondo* and *sonata* and is characterized by vigor and good humor. In short, the *C Major Viola String Quartet* is a crowning masterpiece. Admiration for it increases with familiarity.

WOLFGANG AMADEUS MOZART   (1756–1791)

K. 590   Quartet in F Major

Dedicated to King Friedrich Wilhelm II

The *F Major (K. 590)* string quartet was the last of the 27 quartets which Mozart composed during his lifetime. It was written in the spring of 1790 and is the last one of a series of three quartets dedicated to King Friedrich Wilhelm II of Prussia. This series is known as the Prussian or Berlin quartets. All three quartets in this series were written in major keys – D, B Flat, and F.

Mozart visited Berlin in 1789 at the invitation of the cello–playing monarch, Friedrich Wilhelm II. The King received Mozart with gracious cordiality and offered him a salary of 3,000 thalers (a magnificent stipend at that time) if he would accept the court position of head *kapellmeister*. While considering the offer, Mozart made several appearances as an orchestral conductor at Potsdam. Unfortunately, he succeeded in making himself unpopular by showing his intense dislike for the French musicians in the orchestra and chiefly for Duport, the resident *kapellmeister*. Mozart remarked, "the grinning monsieur (Duport) has been here long enough making German money and eating German bread to be able to speak the German language or at least murder it with his French grimaces." Duport retaliated by starting a repulsive cabal. In the meantime, Mozart became homesick and longed to return to Vienna and to his beloved Constanza. As a consequence, he refused the King's offer, saying, "Am I to leave my good emperor?" The King was touched and is alleged to have said, "Consider my proposal. I shall keep my offer open even if it should be a year before you return to claim it." Before leaving Berlin, the King commissioned Mozart to write six string quartets and six easy piano sonatas for his young daughter, Princess Friedericke. Regrettably, owing to his premature death, Mozart was able to compose only three of the commissioned quartets and only one of the piano sonatas.

The King had an insatiable desire to play string quartets and to display his royal virtuosity as a cellist. In order to please the King, Mozart gave the cello part a predominant role in each of the three quartets, – and particularly in the first two. In the third quartet *(F Major)*, the solo writing for the cello appears only in the first movement. In this quartet, the cello part is integrated with the other instruments in a much more balanced construction than in either the D and B Flat Major quartets.

The first movement, *Allegro moderato*, displays an unusual vigor and intensity. The opening three bars are played in unison by all four instruments. The first bar contains a triad of two half notes played *piano* followed by a unexpected *forte* in a rapidly descending scale. The body of the movement displays majestic melodic phrasing with magnificent instrumental coloring. An unique feature of the movement is the insertion of a *coda* as an ending. After a set of three descending scales played in unison and a brief pause, the first violin and the cello engage in a stubborn dialogue above the rhythmic beats of the second violin and viola. The movement ends with the first violin managing to have the last word.

The second movement, marked *Allegretto* although *Andante* in character, is breath–taking. In the words of Alfred Einstein, the eminent musicologist, this movement is

. . . one of the most sensitive movements in the whole literature of chamber music. It seems to mingle the bliss and sorrow of a farewell to life. How beautiful life has been! How sad! How brief!

The theme of the *Menuetto* is in the form of a peasant dance, known as a Viennese *Teutscher*. (*Teutsch* stands for *Deutsch* in Mozartian dialect.) Unlike the body of the minuet, the trio is in contrast and displays an aristocratic elegance.

The last movement is a typical eighteenth century *Rondo* written in a happy, gay, and light–hearted mood. It is exceptionally evenly balanced with each instrument given an opportunity to display technical virtuosity.

It is not known whether or not King Friedrich Wilhelm II ever received copies of the three string quartets in the series of six which he commissioned. Of the manuscripts, only the *D Major Quartet* was explicitly dedicated by Mozart to the King. It is said that after Mozart's death, the publisher, Artaria, acquired all three quartets "for the price of a sandwich."

CARL AUGUST NIELSEN
Born: June 9, 1865, Sortelung, Island of Funen, Denmark..
Died: October 3, 1931, Copenhagen, Denmark..

CARL AUGUST NIELSEN

Opus 13   Quartet #2 in G Minor

Dedicated to Johan S. Svendsen

I.   *Allegro energico*
II. *Andante amoroso*
III. *Allegro Molto*
IV. *Finale. Allegro (inquieto)*

Carl Nielsen is regarded as Denmark's foremost composer. However, outside of his native land, Nielsen's music was, for the most part, neglected during the first half of this century. It was not until 1950 when the Danish Radio Symphony Orchestra performed Nielsen's *Fifth Symphony* at the Edinburgh Festival that the music community reacted in astonishment that such a monumental work had remained essentially unnoticed for thirty years. Since 1950, there has been a steady *crescendo* of interest in Nielsen's compositions.

During his lifetime, Nielsen wrote six string quartets, two of which were student efforts and remain unpublished. Of the four published quartets, the last one, *Opus 44 in F Major*, is the best known and most popular. This may be due in part to its ready accessibility for purchase. On the other hand, the score and parts of the *G Minor Quartet* are reputed to be out of print.

The opus numbers given by Nielsen for his quartets are misleading. For example, the fourth quartet, *Opus 44*, was originally numbered 19. Nielsen withheld publication of this quartet for twelve years after its first performance and then renumbered it *Opus 44*. Likewise, publication of the *G Minor Quartet*, composed in 1888 at the age of 23, was withheld for a number of years until after the *F Minor, Opus 5 Quartet* had been published. Thus, the *G Minor String Quartet* was Nielsen's first in order of composition although it was second in order of publication.

There is no more severe test of a composer's mastery of polyphony than writing string quartets. Nielsen acquired mastery of this structural form of music early in his career. It is enigmatic that he should have abandoned it during the last twenty–five years of his life. All of Nielsen's string quartets were written before the age of forty.

Carl Nielsen was born of peasant parentage on the Danish island of Fyn. His father played the violin and coronet and was much in demand as a village musician. Carl was taught to play both the violin and coronet by his father and, during his youth, he played in his father's band. With this early musical background, it is only natural that his musical compositions should embrace the simple, uncomplicated songs and provincial dance rhythms of his native island. Nielsen's compositions also reflect the influence of Svendsen, one of his early mentors, and of Brahms for whom he expressed admiration for his talent of teutonic discipline in musical writing.

The first movement of the *G Minor Quartet*, *Allegro energico*, begins with a noble, youthful melody of distinctly Nordic cast and is followed by lively, deft passages. After the recapitulation, there is a changing mood embracing a brief viola and cello duet and ending in an effective *pianissimo*.

The second movement, *Andante amoroso*, is a gentle love song of charm and warmth. The movement is in a mood reminiscent of the well–known violin solo by Svendsen entitled *Romance* (*Opus 26*).

The third movement, marked *Allegro Molto*, is written in *scherzo* form in the key of C Minor and in 6/8 meter. It is essentially a rhythmic, rustic dance. The movement is characteristically Scandinavian in buoyancy and phrasing. The trio in the key of G Major and in 2/4 tempo assumes a charming Schumannesque quality before returning to the original minor key and tempo with *coda*.

The *Finale* designated *Allegro* (*inquieto*) is a restless *rondo* with a lilting rhythm. Toward the close of the movement, Nielsen inserted a *Resume*, which is really a *coda* that combines themes from the first, third, and fourth movements.

String quartets in the category of Nielsen's *G Minor Quartet* are pleasantly attractive and enjoyable if played occasionally at chosen moments. Audiences and players alike are prone to tire of them if they are played too frequently. It is only the sterner stuff of the masters, such as Beethoven's *Opus 59, Number 1*, that can withstand constant repetition with minimal strain.

SERGEI PROKOFIEV
Born: April 23, 1891, Sontsovka, Russia.
Died: March 5, 1953, Moscow, Russia.

SERGEI PROKOFIEV

Opus 92   Quartet # 2 in F Major

Quartet on Kabardinian Themes

I. *Allegro sostenuto*
II. *Adagio*
III. *Allegro*

Prokofiev has long been ranked as one of Russia's most distinguished twentieth century composers. His career has differed from those of his other distinguished colleagues, Shostakovich, Khatchaturian, and Kabalesky, since, unlike them, he did not spend his entire life within the confines of the U.S.S.R. After graduating from the Petrograd Conservatory of Music in 1918, he avoided the revolutionary upheaval in Russia by escaping into the United States. For the next fifteen years, he lived principally in the United States and France. Three of Prokofiev's important compositions were written in our country: (1) *The Love of Three Oranges*, an opera composed for the Chicago Opera Company in 1921; (2) the *Fourth Symphony*, written for the fiftieth anniversary celebration of the Boston Symphony Orchestra and first performed in Boston on November 14, 1930; and (3) the first *String quartet in B Minor, Opus 50*, commissioned by the Elizabeth Sprague Coolidge Foundation of the Library of Congress and first performed at the Library of Congress on April 25, 1931. After a period of deep longing for his homeland, Prokofiev returned to Russia in 1933 to become a Soviet citizen and remained in Russia for the rest of his life.

The bulk of Prokofiev's musical contributions was composed for the theatre and for symphony orchestra performance and piano concerts. His output of chamber music was small, although it has weight. Prokofiev wrote only two string quartets. The second one, like the first, was initiated by extraneous influences.

In August, 1941, when the German armies were rapidly advancing into Russia, a group of Russian artists, including Prokofiev, was evacuated from Moscow to the village of Nalchik, at the foot of Mount Elbrus in the Northern Caucasus between the Black and Caspian Seas. It was here that he became enamoured with the rich folk music of the Kabarda and Balkara tribes in this Mohammedan stronghold of Russia. The primitive dance tunes and rhythms of this region inspired him to compose *String Quartet No. 2*, which he subtitled, *Quartet on Kabardinan Themes*.

Although Prokofiev used the folk songs of the Northern Caucasus as the basis for his second quartet, nevertheless, he transmuted the songs into his own characteristic idiom. Prokofieff had developed a special talent for the transmutation of ethnic themes. For example, in response to a chance request in 1919, he wrote an *Overture on Jewish Themes* for which he received high acclaim for his brilliant craftsmanship. This was a signal tribute since Prokofiev was not of the Jewish faith.

The second quartet is written in classical form with three carefully prepared movements arranged in a manner so that virile, rhythmical sections contrast with the more lyrical, restrained passages. The opening measures of the first movement, *Allegro sostenuto*, start with a war–like rhythm, persistently reiterated in typical Prokofiev style. The accompanying chords are harsh and shocking for a string quartet. The opening theme is followed by melodic passages and is then repeated in the recapitulation.

The second movement, *Adagio*, is en enchanting nocturne. The calm, flowing sounds are decorated with fantastic *arabesques* and are in marked contrast to the brusque effect of the first movement.

The third movement, *Allegro*, is based on the weird, fiery, festive dance music of the Nalchik people. The movement is dominated by the syncopated rhythm of a mountain dance tune called *Getigezhev Ogurbi*.

In our opinion, the major features of *Opus 92* are essentially two–fold: (1) contrasting mixtures of tone colors and rhythms to achieve dramatic impressions, and (2) the introduction of onomatopoeic (*i.e.*, imitative) sound effects. The quartet is regarded as one of the most preeminent compositions in the Soviet repertoire of chamber music.

MAURICE JOSEPH RAVEL
Born: March 7, 1875, Ciboure, France.
Died: December 28, 1937, Paris, France.

276

MAURICE JOSEPH RAVEL

Quator   Quartet in F Major

I.   *Allegro moderato – très doux (F major)*
II. *Assez vif – très rythmé (A minor)*
III. *Très lent (G flat major)*
IV. *Vif et agité (F major)*

In 1899, at the age of 14, Ravel passed the examinations admitting him to the Paris Conservatory of Music where he remained a student for 16 years. Although Ravel was acknowledged as a talented scholar, especially in areas of counterpoint, nevertheless, most of his professors were ill–disposed toward him owing to his arrogant demeanor. He was regarded as *l'enfant terrible*, a revolutionist, a dandy, and certainly a brash non-conformist. Seroff, in his biography of Ravel, states:

> One has to add another peculiar aspect: Ravel seems to have completely ignored the feminine sex. Not even an innocent adolescent feminine infatuation was ever disclosed by those who knew him or was even mentioned by Ravel himself.

Furthermore, he was rejected for military service, to which every young, able–bodied Frenchman was called. With this history and behavioral background, the disposition of the Conservatory authorities was, to some degree, understandable.

As a student, Ravel tried on three occasions to win the competition for the coveted *Prix de Rome*.[1] On his last trial

---

[1]The Academy of France established the *Prix de Rome* in 1666 for the purpose of giving promising French artists an opportunity to devote seven years entirely to the furtherance of their art while living in the Medici Palace in Rome and unencumbered by financial concerns.

in 1902, he submitted the first movement of his string quartet as an entrance requirement and as evidence of his qualifications for the competition. However, this piece did not impress the professorial jury and was judged not to be of a stature worthy of admission even to the preliminary examinations.

By 1902, Ravel was beginning to receive recognition in Parisian musical circles as a promising young composer through the publications of his first two piano compositions, *Pavane pour une Infante defunte* (1899) and *Jeux d'eau* (1901). It is, therefore, not surprising that a wrathful indignation among Ravel's colleagues should develop over the rejection by the Conservatory jury. The indignation reached city–wide proportions after the story became publicized as the "Affaire Ravel" by the two principal Parisian newspapers, *Le Temps* and *Le Matin*. Eventually, the outrage became so bitter that it led to the resignations of Theodore Dubois, the director of the Conservatory, and M. Lenepveu, the leader of the opposition to Ravel. Gabriel Faure, who was Ravel's sympathetic teacher and friend and to whom Ravel had dedicated his quartet, was elected director of the Conservatory to replace Dubois. Although Faure inaugurated many reforms, nevertheless, none of them affected Ravel, and he was obliged to accept with finality his third rejection for the *Prix de Rome*.

Ravel's *String Quartet in F Major* was his first chamber music composition and the only string quartet that he composed during his lifetime. The quartet was modeled after Debussy's quartet, written a decade earlier. A number of critics accused Ravel of plagiarism in the use of Debussy's impressionism as a medium of expression; however,

Debussy himself wrote to Ravel in 1902, "In the name of the gods of music, and of mine, do not alter anything in your quartet." Vincent D'Indy also acclaimed the quartet to be a "piece worthy of any composer's work at the end of a long career." Opinions about the stature of the composition varied considerably during the early years of this century. Even Faure criticized the fourth movement as being "too short and unbalanced." With it all, the quartet did receive an enthusiastic reception in Paris at its first performance by the Heymann Quartet in the hall of the National Music Society on March 5, 1904. Today, Ravel's quartet is established as one of the standard string quartets in the world's literature of chamber music.

The first movement of the quartet, marked *Très doux* (very soft) is written in loose sonata form. It is melodious, easily moving, and is sumptuously rich and colorful. Ravel's feeling for key appears to be modal. One interesting development is the change of key from F Major to D Minor in the middle of the composition with the first violin and viola playing in unison two octaves apart. The last three movements are more daring and are in striking contrast to the singing lyricism of the first movement.

The second movement, *Assez vif – Très rythmé*, bears practically the same designation as the second movement of Debussy's quartet (*Assez vif – bien rythmé*). The quartet is written in 6/8 – 3/4 rhythm and, like the Debussy quartet, makes skillful use of plucked strings. The initial *pizzicato* rhythm is intercepted by a slow middle section. The subsequent return to the initial rhythm evokes a pleasing type of musical expression with a Spanish flavor.

The third movement, designated *Très lent*, is characterized by frequent changes in rhythm from 4/4 to 3/4 and by alterations in keys from A Minor to G Flat Major. These unusual changes create a delicate impressionistic atmosphere. The third movement is, in essence, rhapsodic music of exquisite exotic coloring.

The last movement, marked *Vif et agité* (fast and agitated), is in 5/8 and 3/4 rhythm and alternates from the key of D Minor to F Major. The movement is written in loose rondo form and is characterized by its strikingly unconventional type of rhythm. The movement is conspicuously short. It contains periods of storm and calm and concludes brilliantly in ascending major triads.

Nouvelle Édition revue par l'Auteur

MAURICE RAVEL

à mon cher Maître *GABRIEL FAURÉ*

QUATUOR

Pour 2 Violons, Alto et Violoncelle

ПR

Partition	. . . .
Parties séparées	.
Piano à 2 mains	.
Piano à 4 mains	.
2 Pianos à 4 mains	.

DURAND & Cie, Éditeurs, Paris
4, Place de la Madeleine, 4
United Music Publishers Ltd. Londres.
Elkan-Vogel C°., Philadelphia. Pa (U.S.A.)
Déposé selon les traités internationaux
Propriété pour tous pays.
Tous droits d'exécution, de traduction
de reproductions et d'arrangements réservés
Copyright by Durand et Cie, 1910.
MADE IN FRANCE

Cover from *Quatour* of Ravel.

281

FRANZ PETER SCHUBERT

Born: January 31, 1797, Vienna, Austria.
Died: November 19, 1828, Vienna, Austria.

FRANZ PETER SCHUBERT

Opus 29   Quartet in A Minor

I.   *Allegro ma non troppo*
II. *Andante*
III. *Menuetto allegretto*
IV. *Allegro moderato*

In 1823, after a lapse of three years, Schubert resumed his work of composing string quartets. He had already twelve quartets to his credit. Schubert's return to quartet writing was stimulated to a large degree by Schuppanzigh, a notable Viennese violinist and the leader of the celebrated Schuppanzigh Quartet. The first quartet to emanate from this renewed endeavor was *Quartet No. 13 in A Minor* completed in January or February of 1824. The first performance was given by the Schuppanzigh Quartet on March 15, 1824. It is said that the audience appeared to like the work but that the press was non–committal and that Schubert himself felt the work had been played at a tempo that was too slow. However, the composition was accepted for publication and became available in print in September of the same year. It is noteworthy that his quartet is the only one of Schubert's many masterful compositions of chamber music that was accepted for publication during his lifetime.

The *A Minor Quartet* is one of everybody's favorites owing in large measure to its wealth of melodies. After an introductory accompaniment of two bars, the first movement begins with a melody by the first violin which is suggestive of a song, – especially since it is written within singing range.

The phrase marked "a" represents the main theme written in the key of A Minor. This theme is recapitulated later on in the movement in the key of A Major. The close of the movement, in the form of a *coda*, returns to the key of A Minor.

The second movement, *Andante*, is essentially a transposition to C Major of the Eutr'acte in B Flat Major (Act III) of Schubert's play, *Rosamunde, Fursten von Cypern* (*Rosamund, Princess of Cypress*). This song is one of Schubert's most popular and well–known melodies.

The third movement is a *minuet* and is also related to one of Schubert's songs, *Die Gotter Griechenlands* (*The Gods of Greece*). This song bears the title of one of Schiller's poems from which the text of the song was taken. It begins, "Fair world, where are thou?" The movement has a quality that is both ethereal, mysterious, and metaphysical.

Allegretto

The *finale*, written in the key of A Major, embraces jolly rhythms reminiscent of rural peasant dances. The movement is light–hearted, cheerful, and enchanting. The *Opus 29 Quartet* has brought happiness to a world of music lovers.

FRANZ PETER SCHUBERT (1798–1828)

Opus 125, No. 1 Quartet in E Flat Major

I.   *Allegro Moderato*
II. *SCHERZO Prestissimo*
III. *Adagio*
IV. *Allegro*

The two string quartets that comprise *Opus 125* (*E Flat Major* and *E Major*) are listed as quartet numbers 10 and 11. They were written in the years 1813 to 1814 and 1817, respectively. These early quartets were composed principally for home entertainment (*gebrauchsmusik*). They included sprightly, happy melodies and are obviously designed to please both players and listeners.

The *E Flat Quartet* is written in *sonata* form. The first movement contains effective four part instrumentation with periods in which two instruments are set against the other. The short *scherzo* and *trio* (E Flat and C Minor) in the second movement have been humorously contrived. The unique calls in the *scherzo* movement are believed to indicate Schubert's schoolboy prank of inserting donkey brays into an otherwise serious composition. The contrast between the first and second movements is striking.

For the third movement (*Adagio*), Schubert adhered to the original key of E Flat Major. The theme of this movement is exalted and heavenly. The subject material has a religious cast and would have been appropriate for a *Sanctus*. The *Finale*, without any change of key, is vivacious and written in a grandiose *rondo* style. It is a first violinist's delight, owing to the enchanting solos.

Schubert's tenth quartet is notable for its clarity and youthful esprit. Obviously, it cannot be compared with the intellectual sophistication of the monumental fifteenth quartet, *G Major, Opus 161*, – written a decade later.

Birthplace of Franz Peter Schubert, Vienna, Austria.

FRANZ PETER SCHUBERT (1797–1828)

Opus Posthumous Quartet in D Minor

Death and the Maiden

I.   *Allegro*
II. *Andante con moto*
III. *Scherzo. Allegro molto*
IV. *Presto – prestissimo*

In 1817, at the age of 20, Schubert wrote a number of songs, one of which was based on a poem by Mathias Claudius entitled *Death and the Maiden*. The poem presents a dialogue between Death and a Maiden. The Maiden pleads for Death to pass her by. Death explains that he is a friend and that he has come not to punish her but to soothe her so that she may sleep gently in his arms. Seven years later, in 1824, Schubert recalled his musical dramatization of the Claudius poem and decided to incorporate the song as the main theme in the *Andante* movement of the *D Minor Quartet*, the fourteenth in this series of quartets. The quartet immediately became known as the *Death and the Maiden*.

There appears to be no doubt that in the spring of 1824, Schubert suffered a mild depression and became obsessed with thoughts of death. This is evident from the contents of his letters and from the choice of texts used in his compositions, *i.e., Bei dem Grabe meines Vater (At the Grave of my Father)* by Claudius; *der Jungling an den Tod (The Youth Speaks to Death)* by Spaun; *Gruppe aus dem Tartarus (A Group in Hades)* based upon a poem by Schiller; *Am Grabe Anselmos (At Anselm's Grave)* by Claudius. The inevitability of death appears to have transfixed Schubert's innermost thoughts into musical sounds.

Although it will never be known what Schubert had in mind when he wrote the *D Minor Quartet*, nevertheless its association with the Claudius poem undoubtedly influenced its interpretation and has given rise to years of speculation.

Cobbett[1] quotes Huess'[2] interpretations of the various movements. In brief, it is speculated that the struggle with Death is the subject of the first movement. The second movement is perceived to portray Death's words and the variations to depict Death as a friend. The ending is regarded as one of resignation. According to Huess, the *Scherzo* movement portrays Death as a demon fiddler. This movement is in marked contrast to the ethereal ending of the *Andante* movement. Quoting from Cobbett:

The finale is most definitely in the character of a dance of death; ghastly visions whirl past in the inexorable uniform rhythm of the tarantella.[3]

---

[1]Cobbett's *Cyclopedic Survey of Chamber Music*. Oxford University Press, 1930.

[2]Huess, Alfred V.: *Kammermusik Abende*. Breitkopf and Hartel, Leipzig, 1919.

[3]In the country surrounding the seaport city, Taranto, Italy, a spider may be found which is called a *tarantula*. The bite of this spider was supposed to cause a disease called *tarantism*. During the Middle Ages, this malady (probably mostly hysteria [FWS]) was alleged to be curable by the playing of a fast, lively dance tune called the *tarantella*. Pepys, in 1662, records his meeting with a gentleman who "is a great traveller and, speaking of the *taranula*, he says that all the harvest long (about which time they are most busy) there are fiddlers going up and down the fields everywhere in expectation of being hired by those that are stung.

The *D Minor Quartet* is unusually lengthy. The four movements with repetition cover 1,953 measures. Even in the first performance at the Schwarzenberg Palace in Vienna on February 1, 1826, and in the composer's presence, cuts were made since the quartet was acknowledged to be too long. Later, twenty years after Schubert's death, the Hellmesberger Quartet, the most prestigious quartet in Europe at that time, not only made cuts in the quartet but also tossed off light pieces by other composers in between movements in order to dispel the gloom. The somber, reflective character of the quartet is reinforced by the use of minor modes in all four movements, – D Minor, G Minor, D Minor, and D Minor. Schubert offered the quartet to Schott, the publisher, in 1828, but Schott refused to accept it. The quartet was eventually published three years after Schubert's death by the Czerny publishing house. Robert Schumann called the *D Minor Quartet* the best consolation that has been given to us for the composer's early demise.

The *D Minor Quartet* opens with a demanding call for attention. This is followed by a bold rhythmic exposition. The subject matter is at first promulgated by rhythmic triplet passages that eventually modulate into sixteenth note suspensions. The movement closes with a quiet *piu mosso* section reminiscent of the opening exposition and a return to the original tempo.

The *Andante* movement consists of five variations on the *Tod und das Madchen* theme. The movement opens solemnly in a firm, slow–marching tempo with all four instruments playing in the middle register to produce a mournful, funereal effect. This is followed by a variation in which the first violin plays convoluted twists and turns in the higher register above the other three voices. The effect may be characterized as that of a ballerina sprightly dancing in the midst of doleful surroundings. This variation is succeeded by a galloping rhythm in which it is "tempting to hear Death riding his horse and carrying off the Maiden". In the minds of most listeners, the variations emerge pictorially. The movement closes with a whispering version of the opening melody.

Both the *Scherzo* and the *finale* are in the character of the dance of death. The *finale* contains brief brooding fragments from Schubert's *Erlkonig*; however, in the main it is a frenzied dance of death. The *finale* closes with a *prestissimo coda*.

In Cobbett's words:

The importance of the D minor quartet lies. . . not only in its spiritual quality (but) in the inner force of cohesion which welds all four instruments into a unity under the pressure of a dominating idea – the dance of death.

FRANZ PETER SCHUBERT (1797–1828)

Quartettsatz   C Minor

I.   Allegro assai

The *Quartettsatz* is a fragmentary masterpiece which Schubert wrote in December 1820. The last of Schubert's youthful quartets was written in 1817. The early quartets were composed in the classical style after the mode of the *Opus 18* Beethoven quartets to which Schubert had become enamored. The *Quartettsatz* represents a complete break away from the classical style of the earlier period.

The movement of *Quartettsatz* begins with a mystical tremolo followed by restless eighth note passages for the first violin. A peaceful melody is then interjected for the next 36 bars, which is again followed by an agitated passage. Schubert displays his genius of introducing simplistic harmonies as mere whispers (*ppp*).

There are then recapitulations with a *tremolo* at the ending to supply the concluding tragic notes.

Schubert obviously intended to write a second movement to the quartet since a sketch of 16 bars has been located. What a loss to the world of chamber music!

The autographed score of *Quartettsatz in C Minor* was found among Brahms's possessions. This quartet was first published in Leipzig in 1870 by B. Senff.

DIMITRI SHOSTAKOVICH
Born: September 25, 1906, Saint Petersburg, Russia.
Died: August 9, 1975, Moscow, Russia.

DIMITRI SHOSTAKOVICH

Opus 108   Quartet # 7

I.   *Allegretto*
II. *Lento*
III. *Allegro*

The seventh quartet of Shostakovich is the shortest of his fifteen quartets. The three movements of the quartet are played without interruption and are somewhat similar in dimension and character to the well–known first quartet, *Opus 49*. The *F Sharp Minor Quartet* was written in 1960 and dedicated to the memory of Shostakovich's first wife, Nina Vashyevna, with whom he spent twenty–six years of his life from 1929 to 1955.

The first movement contains no developmental section and leaps from a grotesque dance theme in 2/4 rhythm with occasional 3/4 interjections to a theme with 3/8 rhythm, played *pizzicato*. The movement, which gives a feeling of pathos, finally returns to the original rhythm and dies away with percussion chords.

The *Lento* movement begins with a muted song in high register by the first violin accompanied by soft *arpeggios* from the second violin. In this movement, Shostakovich transposed the melody from F Sharp Minor to C Major. In the last movement, the themes of the first two movements are brought together, and the four voices participate in a raging *fugue*. About halfway through the movement, the music changes abruptly into a muted waltz by the first violin, – bespeaking a feeling of sad loneliness. As the waltz fades away, the *pizzicato* theme of the first movement reappears. The quartet is distinguished by the masterly manner with which unification of the themes is achieved.

The quartet was written during a period in which Shostakovich suffered from loneliness. His friends had either died or disappeared, his beloved wife had passed away, and his children became independent. A second, unhappy marriage to Margarita Kainova ended quickly in a divorce. For Shostakovich, the world had turned gray, and he sought contentment by composing privately. The seventh quartet bears the scars of this period.

Памяти …чы Васильевны Шостакович

СЕДЬМОЙ КВАРТЕТ

Д. ШОСТАКОВИЧ
Соч.108 (1960г)

I

Allegretto ♩=120

Советский композитор   C 2020 к
Москва 1960

Printed in USSR

Score – Shostakovich, *Opus 108.*

295

BEDŘICH SMETANA
Born: March 2, 1824, Litomysl, Bohemia (now Czechoslovakia).
Died: May 12, 1884, Prague, Czechoslovakia.

296

BEDŘICH SMETANA

Quartet No. 1   **E Minor**

Aus meinem Leben *(From My Life)*

I.   *Allegro vivo appassionato*
II. *Allegro moderato a la Polka*
III. *Largo Sostenuto*
IV. *Vivace*

Smetana's name was so frequently mispronounced that he quoted the closing bars of the *Minuet* movement of Beethoven's violin and piano sonata, *Opus 30, No. 3*, to provide the correct accent:

Smetana will largely be remembered as the founder of Czech nationalism in the field of music.

As a boy, Smetana is said to have rivaled Mozart as a child prodigy. At the age of six years, he made a public debut as a pianist, and, at the age of eight years, he composed several dance melodies. His early life was filled with many hardships which helped to turn his ambitions from virtuosity to composition.

297

At the encouragement of Liszt, Smetana opened a private music school in Prague in 1849. From this beginning, Smetana led the way through his creative faculties to furthering Czech opera. Smetana composed a series of eight patriotic operas, the first of which was *The Brandenburgers*, composed in 1863. This opera, produced in 1866, was enthusiastically received. It was subsequently eclipsed by the overwhelming popularity of the *Bartered Bride*. Smetana stimulated the Czechs to take a national pride in their musical accomplishments. His compositions are loved and known throughout Czechoslovakia. A centenary festival of his birth was celebrated in March 1924.

Smetana composed the *String Quartet in E Minor* in 1876 at the age of 52 years. This is one of his two principal works in chamber music, – the other being the *G Minor Piano Trio* written 21 years previously (1855) in memory of the loss of his son, Bedriska. The intervening years between these two outstanding compositions not only witnessed Smetana's acceptance as a national musician in Bohemia but also included periods of mental and physical distress. Two years before the quartet was composed, Smetana became deaf and was forced to seek refuge with his daughter in the quiet woodland of Jabkenice. It was while resting at his daughter's home that he struck upon the idea of composing a work that was autobiographical and would depict his life. In a letter dated April 12, 1878 to a friend, Joseph Srb, Smetana gave a detailed explanation of the *Quartet in E Minor*:

My intention was to depict in music the course of my life.
1st movement: Drawn to art during my youth, romantic mood,

298

inexpressible longing. . . . At the same time, even at that early stage, warning of the affliction to come and the long–held note, a very high E, from the *Finale*; this is the ominous shrill whistling which began to sound in my ears in 1874, and led to my deafness. . . . The 2nd movement: *Quasi Polka*, takes me back in memory to the cheerful life of my youth, when as a composer I poured out a stream of dances, and was myself known as an enthusiastic dancer, etc. . . . The 3rd movement, *Largo sostenuto*, reminds me of the happiness of my first love for a young girl, who later became my faithful wife. The 4th movement: recognition of the elemental power of national music, satisfaction at the success of the course my life had taken until the moment of sudden interruption owing to the ominous catastrophe – the onset of deafness, a joyless future outlook, a faint glimmer of hope of improvement, but finally only a sense of pain. That is the approximate content of the composition, which is of a private character and was therefore written for only four instruments; they discuss all that has had an important bearing on my life as though they were a group of close friends. That is all.

Cobbett notes that the high E on the violin in the *finale* movement of the quartet provides "one of the saddest moments in all chamber music." Smetana wrote:

It is the fatal sounding in my ear of the high–pitched tones which in 1874 announced to me my approaching deafness.

The quartet, *From My Life*, is an intensely introspective composition which disturbed him mentally and finally led to insanity.

From an engraving by C. Calcinoto.

GIUSEPPE TARTINI

Born: April 8, 1692, Pirano, Istria.
Died: February 26, 1770, Padua, Italy.

GIUSEPPE TARTINI

Sonata   G Minor

Dido Forsaken

I.   *Adagio*
II. *Non troppo presto*
III. *Largo; Allegro commodo*

Tartini was born in Pirano and died in Padua. The son of a wealthy Italian nobleman, Tartini was educated by turns for the church, the law, and the army. During his youth, he became a champion fencer and a skillful violinist. After spending a period in hiding and study in the monastery in Assisi, he settled in Padua and spent a glorious career as a concert violinist, teacher, and composer.

During his lifetime, Tartini composed more than 40 violin sonatas and at least 13 concertos. The best known and deservedly the most popular works of Tartini are two sonatas, both written in the key of G minor, and entitled, respectively, the *Devil's Trill* and *Dido Forsaken*.[1]

The first movement, *Adagio*, is in 8/8 rhythm and demands a warm, lovely tone in order to convey the sorrowful character of its music. Likewise, the scale passages require a mixed variation of tonal color to express their beauty. The movement ends in a majestic *forte*.

---

[1]Dido was a Tyrian princess and reputed to be the founder and queen of Carthage. In Virgil's *Aeneid*, Dido fell in love with Aeneid; however, Aeneid eventually deserted her. Thus abandoned and forsaken, Dido committed suicide by stabbing herself on a funeral pyre.

The second movement is passionate and tempestuous. The *arpeggio* passages are dominated by mordent accents and flying *staccati* with a light bow.

The third movement begins with a *Largo* introduction followed by the main *Allegro Commodo* section. This movement is imbued with a soulful, melodious spirit coupled with melancholy tonal color. The movement closes *forte piu lento*.

Sonata in G minor

I

G. TARTINI
Violin Part Edited by
LEOPOLD AUER

21204ᵇ 37

Score – Tartini, *Sonata in G Minor*.

PETER ILITCH TCHAIKOVSKY
Born: May 7, 1840, Kamsko–Votinsk, Russia.
Died: November 6, 1893, Saint Petersburg, Russia.

PETER ILITCH TCHAIKOVSKY

Opus 11   Quartet in D Major

I.   *Moderato e Semplice*
II. *Andante Cantabile*
III. *Scherzo, Allegro non Tanto*
IV. *Finale, Allegro Giusto*

Nowadays, Tchaikovsky is best known for his orchestral compositions; however, during his lifetime his chamber music works were more dominant. They were also more influential in establishing his reputation as a composer than his symphonies, tone–poems, and concertos. Although Tchaikovsky's contributions to chamber music are relatively few, nevertheless, they are substantial, elegant, unique, and distinctly Russian.

Nicholas Rubinstein founded the Music Conservatory of Moscow in 1866 and enlisted Tchaikovsky, at the age of 26, to serve as the Professor of Harmony and Counterpoint. The salary was low, but the position was an honorable one and allowed Tchaikovsky ample time to follow his heart's desire to compose music.

The circumstances that led Tchaikovsky to compose his first string quartet are distressing. In the summer of 1879, Rubinstein lost his money at roulette, and the Conservatory became desperate for cash. Curtailment of funds reached uncomfortable proportions and led Rubinstein to suggest that Tchaikovsky raise money by giving a concert of his own compositions. In order to present a balanced concert, it was essential that a work of classical dimensions be included in the program. Since it was too costly to engage an orchestra for the occasion, Tchaikovsky decided to compose a string quartet and to obtain the services of colleagues to perform the work.[1]

Tchaikovsky spent the entire month of February 1871 composing the *Opus 11* string quartet for the concert to be given on March 28. The concert was given as scheduled and proved to be a huge success. Both the audience and the reviewers were enthusiastic in their response to the program and, in particular, to the string quartet. Laroche, one of the reviewers, described the string quartet as:

. . . distinguished by the same succulent melodies, beautifully and interestingly harmonized, the same nobility of tone. . . and the same slightly feminine softness to which we have become accustomed in this gifted composer.

The slow movement, Andante Cantabile, received special recognition. The melody was derived from a folk tune that Tchaikovsky had heard a carpenter sing on a visit to Kamenka in the province of Kiev.[2] The *Andante Cantabile* soon achieved international fame and eventually underwent a wide variety of transcriptions for all sorts of instrumental combinations, – even including swing orchestras and a solo for double bass with piano accompaniment. The popularity of this melody, however, did not in any way diminish its innate beauty when played by the four instruments for which it was originally scored.

---

[1]A quartet was organized under the name of the Russian Music Society Quartet. The members were Ferdinand Laub, a Czeck violinist and Professor of Violin at the Conservatory; Pryanishnikov, a Russian violinist; Aloysius Minkus, the ballet composer and violist; and the well–known German 'cellist, Wilhelm Karl Friedrich Fitzenhagen.

[2]The words of the folk song are doggerel, – "Vanya sat drinking and as he drank he thought of his sweetheart."

The immediate international appeal for Tchaikovsky's first quartet was not entirely attributable to the melodious *Andante Cantabile*. The themes of the entire quartet captivated the world. The first edition of the quartet became exhausted in 1875, and the Moscow publisher, Jurgenson, speedily printed a second one. As evidence of the international appeal, it may be noted that at the time of the second printing, only eleven copies of the first edition had been sold in Russia and all of the other copies had been sold abroad.

Tchaikovsky dedicated the first quartet to his botanist friend and librettist, Professor Sergey A. Rachinsky.

The first movement, *moderato e semplice*, is the longest movement in the quartet. It is written in *sonata* form and in 9/8 rhythm. The beginning cast in a sketch of harmonic syncopations, as shown in the example.

The exposition is then followed by a beautiful lamenting *largamente* passage and closes with a highly imaginative *poco piu mosso* section. (See example on next page.)

The movement continues with repetitions in which the first violin is engaged in a series of configurations against the syncopated rhythms of the other three instruments. The conclusion begins with a recapitulation of the *poco piu mosso* theme which is extended into an *Allegro giusto coda* and then into a brisk *poco accelerando* dash to the end.

The famous *Andante Cantabile* in B flat major with muted strings is essentially in ternary form. The theme is strikingly beautiful and graceful in its simplicity. The trio is especially soulful with its two introductory bars followed by a gently, expressive motif accompanied by the cello playing pianissimo pizzicato. The work was included in a concert given at the Moscow Conservatory in 1877 honoring the novelist and philosopher, Count Lev Nikolaevich Tolstoi (1828–1910). Commenting on the occasion, Tchaikovsky wrote in his diary,

Never in my life have I felt so flattered and proud of my creative ability as when Lev Tolstoi, sitting next to me, heard my Andante with tears coursing down his cheeks.

The third movement, *Scherzo Allegro non tanto* in D minor, is Schumannesque in style. It is lively, rhythmical, and appealing. The opening passage is shown in the example on the next page.

Allegro non tanto

The *Finale, Allegro giusto,* similar to the first movement, is written in sonata form in the key of D Major. The first theme in the *Finale* is bright and cheery.

Allegro giusto

Finale

The second theme is typically Russian in character. The *Finale* movement continues with the themes repeated in ingenious developments and closes *Allegro vivace* in a whirl of fragments taken from the initial passage.

Tchaikovsky's death was untimely at the age of 53. The official record attributed his death to cholera; however, it is generally held that death was self–inflicted during one of his frequent periods of melancholia.

GIUSEPPI VERDI
Born: October 10, 1813, Le Roncole, Italy.
Died: January 27, 1901, Milan, Italy.

310

GIUSEPPI VERDI

Quartet   E Minor

I.   *Allegro*
II. *Andantino*
III. *Prestissimo*
IV. *Scherzo–Fuga*

The *E Minor Quartet* is Verdi's sole contribution to chamber music literature. The quartet was written in March, 1873, during a period of enforced leisure. Verdi had gone to Naples to attend the rehearsals of his opera, *Aida*. The *prima donna*, Theresa Stolz, who had been engaged to sing the title role, suddenly fell ill, and the production had to be postponed. While waiting for the singer's recovery, Verdi amused himself by composing a string quartet "to pass the time." The quartet was performed soon after its completion at the Albergo delle Crocelle in Naples in the presence of a few intimate friends. Initially, Verdi regarded the quartet as "of no importance" and refused to have it printed or performed publicly. Later, he relented and permitted the quartet to be played in Paris in 1876 and to be published by Schott in 1877.

The quartet is constructed along classical lines and conventional rules of harmony. The themes display Verdi's exceptional gift for melody. Operatic *devotees* will be able to identify fragments of operatic *arias* that are incorporated throughout the quartet.

The tranquil theme of the first movement is announced by the second violin and is then repeated by the first violin accompanied by the other instruments. An early dramatic effect is attained when all voices play *incalzando* (pressing forward) *fortissimo* in cadence. Further dramatic effects are produced by the interjection of rapid cross melodies. The second theme in the movement is also pleasingly tranquil and finally leads into a repetition of the first subject.

The second movement (*Andantino*) carries a simple, catchy, whistling melody. It is the one tune most likely to be readily recalled.

The *Prestissimo* of the third movement is of typical operatic character. The trio in A Major is a cello solo in the nature of an operatic *aria* accompanied by plucked strings in the other instruments.

The final *Scherzo–Fuga* is no doubt the most sophisticated movement of the quartet. The colorful themes are mortised into a firm, persistent rhythm and provide a study in hermeneutics (*i.e.*, interpretations). For some, the rapid passages will suggest the twitter of birds; for others, they depict the rapid chatter of the women in *Falstaff*.

In our opinion, the Verdi quartet is not great music when compared to the quartets of Beethoven and Brahms. However, the quartet certainly merits occasional performance since it supplies listening pleasure.

2

QUARTETT

VIOLINE I

Giuseppe Verdi
(1813-1901)

Edition Peters N° 4255

10945

Violin I – Verdi, *Quartet in E Minor.*

313

ANTON VON WEBERN
Born: December 3, 1883, Vienna, Austria.
Died: September 15, 1945, Mittersill, Austria.

ANTON VON WEBERN

Rondo for String Quartet

(C. 1906)

Webern, one of the earliest pupils of Arnold Schonberg, followed his teacher's methods during the first part of this century by adopting atonality and serialism as characteristics of his music compositions. Let it be noted, however, that Webern was not an imitator but pursued his work with autonomy and originality. Webern and his compatriot, Alban Berg, another Schonberg disciple, soon became identified with Schonberg's ultramodern school of music composition and formed a lasting friendship with their revered mentor. The triumvirate of Schonberg, Webern, and Berg became universally recognized, criticized, and extolled as musical reformers. Unfortunately, their concerted activities were prematurely disrupted by death and World War II. As a result of the political environment in the 1930s, Schonberg, a Jew, emigrated to Los Angeles. On the other hand, Webern and Berg, both Catholics, remained in Austria. Berg died of a staphylococcal (?) septicemia in 1935, and Webern met a tragic death in 1945. Five months after the termination of war hostilities, Webern was shot to death by a trigger–nervous American soldier. The circumstances of the tragedy have been disclosed in a carefully documented book.[1] Schonberg outlived both of his students and died in 1951.

---

[1]Moldenhauer, Hans: *The Death of Anton Webern: A Drama in Documents.* New York. Philosophical Library, 1961, 118 pp.

Great credit accrues to Hans Moldenhauer, a faculty member of the University of Washington in Seattle, for organizing the first International Webern Festival in 1962 and for establishing in this country a comprehensive archive of primary source materials relating to Anton Webern. The manner by which the Pacific Northwest of these United States, 7,000 miles distant from Webern's native Vienna, became the respository of the Webern Archive is interestingly delineated in a book entitled *Anton von Webern Perspectives*.[2] The Webern Archive consists of a comprehensive collection of musical manuscripts, plays, diaries, letters, documents, photographs, Webern's reference library, personal relics, objects of art, essays, programs, newspaper accounts, scores, recordings, and related materials.

Webern's musical output was relatively sparce. Krenek points out that there is no musical composer of comparable stature whose entire life's work takes no more than three hours of performance time. Of Webern's thirty–one numbered works, only his last composition, a *cantata*, takes a little more than ten minutes to perform. His shortest composition lasts less than two minutes. Much of his music is fragile and delicate in texture with every note carefully weighed. Although Webern's music was, for the most part, despised during his lifetime, nevertheless following his unfortunate death, Webern's influence spread with incredible speed. The reason that listeners are fascinated and moved by Webern's compositions is usually

---

[2]Compiled by Hans Moldenhauer; edited by Demas Irvine; and published by the University of Washington Press, Seattle, 1966.

attributed to the intensity of his musical concentration. It has been said that Webern was capable of distilling his musical matter into "a few drops of precious essence."

The *Rondo for String Quartet* (*c.* 1906) is an early work that appears to have been composed between his *Quartet in A Minor* and the *Sonatensatz* for piano. During this early period (before Schonberg's influence), Webern adopted a Brahmsian style for his compositions. Webern's major move from tonality to atonality did not occur until 1908–1909.

The *Rondo* is a one movement *quartetsatz*. It is a moving melody, – written in the key of F and in 6/8 tempo. The quartet follows a traditional classical and romantic form. In this respect, it is reminiscent of Schonberg's lyrical 1897 *String Quartet in D Major, Opus 1.*

There is comparatively little information available about the *Rondo* quartet. The work is included as an unnumbered opus in the Webern Archive at the University of Washington. It appears to have been first performed in Hanover, New Hampshire, August 1, 1968, by the Philadelphia String Quartet. The *Rondo* quartet was edited by Wallace McKenzie and published by the Carl Fisher Company in 1970.

HUGO WOLF
Born: March 13, 1860, Windischgraz, Austria (now Yugoslavia).
Died: February 22, 1903, Vienna, Austria.

HUGO WOLF

Italian Serenade   G Major

I.   *Molto Vivo*

Hugo Wolf will always be remembered as an Austrian song writer. He wrote only one string quartet which was essentially a youthful experiment and is no longer available.

The *Italian Serenade* for string quartet is an arrangement that Wolf made from his orchestral composition bearing the same name. The arrangement was first performed in Vienna posthumously in 1904 and since then has been favorably received.

Music soothes us, stirs us up; it puts noble feelings in us;
it melts us to tears, we know not how; — it is a language by itself,
just as perfect, in its way, as speech, as words; just as divine,
just as blessed. . . . Music has been called the speech of angels;
I will go further, and call it the speech of God himself.

Charles Kingsley (1819–1875)

The Author

Dr. F. William Sunderman Sr. is a world–renowned physician, pathologist, clinical scientist, toxicologist, author, editor, and a life–long violinist. He is presently Director of the Institute for Clinical Science, Pennsylvania Hospital, Philadelphia, Pennsylvania, and Director of Education for the Association of Clinical Scientists, of which he was founder and first president. He is also the editor of *Annals of Clinical and Laboratory Science*. He is Emeritus Professor of Pathology, Hahnemann University Medical School and Honorary Clinical Professor of Medicine, Jefferson Medical College, – both in Philadelphia. He is a Past President of the American Society of Clinical Pathologists. He served as a Founding Governor of the College of American Pathologists and is a Life Trustee of the American Board of Pathology. During World War II, he served as the Medical Director of Division 8 of the Office of Scientific Research and Development.

Dr. Sunderman has been the recipient of many national and international awards. They include U.S.A. Naval Ordinance Development Award; Medal of Honor, Armed Forces institute of Pathology; citation from the Japanese government for medical aid to workers exposed to nickel carbonyl in Nagoya; Honorary Membership in the British Association of Clinical Biochemists; Distinguished Service Cross, Order of Merit, Federal Republic of Germany; Lifetime Achievement Award, Joint Congresses of the IX Congresso Nacional de la Societad Espanola de Quimica Clinica, the Second International Congress of Therapeutic Drug Monitoring and Toxicology, and the Fourth International Congress on Automation and New Technology, Spain; Lifetime Honors Award in Nickel Toxicology, International Union of Pure and Applied Chemistry, Finland; Diploma de Honor, Latinamericano de Bioquimica Clinica, Venezuela; Guest lecturer at Beijing University Medical College, People's Republic of China; Ward Burdick Award, given jointly by the American Society of Clinical Pathologists and the College of American Pathologists; Pathologist of the Year Award, College of American Pathologists, Gold–headed Cane Award, Association of Clinical Scientists; John Gunther Rheinhold Award and Award for Outstanding Contributions to Clinical Chemistry in Education, American Association of Clinical Chemistry.

Biographical citations for Dr. Sunderman are listed in *Who's Who, Who's Who in America, Who's Who in the World, American Men of Science, Directory of Medical Specialists, Men of Achievement, Dictionary of International Biography, La Societe Internationale de Who's Who, The International Blue Book of World Notables,* and *International Who's Who in Music.*

Dr. Sunderman served as violin soloist during his youth in the summer Chautauqua concerts. In recent years, he has been a guest soloist in "Senior Artists Showcase," Concerto Soloists, Philadelphia; in "Unstrung Heroes" recitals, Concerto Soloists; violin soloist at String Teachers Workshop Orchestra concerts; guest participant with the Märkl String Quartet; and participant in Carnegie Hall, New York, concert under the auspices of the International Congress on Arts and Medicine (1992). He is the founder of the Sunderman Foundation for Chamber Music at Gettysburg College.

M. L. S.